Advance Praise for *Positively Conflicted*

I started and ran two organizations that collectively published hundreds of books that I personally green-lighted, and I've written almost a score of books myself. Yet rarely, if ever, have I found a book as searingly insightful, engaging, profound, and practical all at once. What's more, the topic itself—which hones in on the essence of interpersonal relationships and their connections to the inner workings of each individual—is extraordinarily relevant and essential to all of our lives.

> —*Alan Blankstein, founder of the HOPE foundation, New York*

A practical guide to letting go of fear and its traveling companion, control, to corral conflict and enhance interpersonal relationships—from the bedroom to the boardroom. Could even make you a better citizen along the way.

> —*Bonnie Gibson, former partner and immigration lawyer at Fragomen Worldwide Immigration Attorneys, Phoenix, Arizona*

Praise for Sam Ardery

Sam's approach to mediation is centered first on people and not solely on the dispute. I have benefited from Sam's thoughtful, direct, and concise approach, and his resolution skills are immediately recognizable. It is rare to find a person who has so many natural traits to help people work through life's intense challenges by calling upon their personal character and dignity.

> —*Dan Cates, PhD, former superintendent of schools, High School District 211, Palatine, Illinois*

Sam has the wisdom to see when situations that we encounter and that need to be resolved are crowded out by our fear and anger. Sam has enough sense of self to not be afraid to ask hard questions and risk challenging you if he thinks it will help you resolve a complex issue.

> —*Ray McKinnon, Academy-Award-winning writer, Los Angeles*

Sam Ardery has been a friend of mine for fifty years. We share similar roots and common values. We have spent many hours together, sometimes talking and sometimes silent, but always appreciating each other's presence. Sam is a skilled listener who embraces the role of confidant and adviser. He is genuinely kind and compassionate, and I have relied heavily on his advice throughout our many years of friendship.

—*David Theil, MD, chair of anesthesiology,*
Rose Medical Center, Denver

I have known Sam since the mid-80s, and it has been an absolute privilege and pleasure. Sam is as fine a man as they come. Beyond his great personality, soft-spoken way, and boyish smile, Sam is an incredible lawyer and problem solver. On a personal note, Sam is a dedicated family man with fine values and a strong spiritual life. I consider Sam to be a great friend and a caring individual.

—*Bob Deacy, environmental scientist,*
West Palm Beach, Florida

Over the years, what I have consistently appreciated most about Sam is that he is *so* genuine. In thought, conversation, and actions, he is able to come alongside *someone* and bring real wisdom, insight, and compassion in such an affirming way. I always leave our "coffee conversations" refreshed and challenged. He's an amazing person.

—*Karen Adams, EdD, chief of staff, office of the president,*
Indiana University, Bloomington, Indiana

How might Sam approach a problem…personal or professional? Well, two things come to mind—honesty and compassion. Sam is able to have hard conversations in an effective way due to his forthright and at times painfully honest diagnosis of the problem as well as the often difficult solution he offers. He keeps the best interest of his client/friend in mind with such dealings and, despite the challenge of an honest approach, he is skillful in delivering his solutions in caring and compassionate ways. And it's authentic. I can attest to this as I've known him most of his life and have observed him in action of all sorts. There's no pretense, very little personal interest of gain, and a sincere interest in a good outcome.

—*Andy Karozos, MD, integrative medicine and acupuncture, Healdsburg, California*

Sam Ardery teaches negotiation skills in a way that makes you re-evaluate your professional tactics, but he also transforms the way you think about your personal and day-to-day interactions. There is a lot of literature available about negotiation techniques, but Sam Ardery takes that body of knowledge and boils it down into straight-forward and practical steps that can be used to approach both complex and everyday problems.

—*Caitlin J. Nelson, former law student, Chicago*

Be prepared! When you meet Sam, you will likely feel an immediate sense of calm and trust. He has that effect on people. He is an engaging, curious listener and teacher and, dare I say, a master of the hard conversation.

—*Tim Orbaugh, PhD, entrepreneur consultant, Tucson*

2-10-2023

Julie,

If you read a portion of this book, I
hope you find value.

Warm regards,

Sam

Positively Conflicted

Engaging with Courage, Compassion,
and Wisdom in a Combative World

Sam Ardery

Maxwell Lane Press

Published by Maxwell Lane Press
3340 North Lawndale Ave. 1N
Chicago, IL 60618

ISBN: 978-1-7362949-0-1 (paperback)
ISBN: 978-1-7362949-1-8 (ebook)
LCCN: 2020925288

For Patty

Be joyful though you have considered all the facts.
—Wendell Berry, *Manifesto: The Mad Farmer Liberation Front*

Contents

Foreword

I met Sam Ardery in 1976 in Greencastle, Indiana. We were freshmen in college. Over the four years we did typical things friends did: we went to a dance; we studied together for economics. We had grandmothers who lived in the same small town in Indiana, who went to the same church, and bragged about us. Sam and I ended up going to the same law school and sharing a friend group. We have kept our friendship going through the years, albeit at times there were long lapses. When Sam asked me to consider writing a foreword for his book, I was both honored and humbled. I wondered what I could say that would be remotely meaningful. Then I read his book. This book sounds *exactly* like Sam; it is as if I am sitting at Au Bon Pain, having a cup of coffee with him, and we are wrestling with how conflict plays out in our lives.

Sam challenges readers by courageously sharing his own story. His story is honest and demonstrates vulnerability; in so doing he models for readers both the importance of our own stories and the importance of exploring our own fears, biases, and stereotypes. He wants us to consider what it would be like to embrace conflict instead of avoiding it, to acknowledge that my version of the facts is just that—my version. Through stories, he allows readers to get beyond the exhausting scorekeeping of *how often I am right* and challenges us to consider why we need to be right and what fears lie underneath that need.

This book gently invites readers to jump into an adventure and to reframe how conflict plays out in our lives. At my work we spend a lot of energy talking about how to deal with conflict and the importance of candid, direct conversations. My office bookshelf is filled with a wide array of excellent resources to help leaders think through how to prepare for and conduct conversations where there are differing, conflicting, points of view. These books focus on the important work that needs to be done to arrive at a resolution of a conflict that will allow the parties to feel heard and valued and able to move on. In my view, *Positively Conflicted* brings a much-needed and very different lens to addressing conflict—it begins with the individual. The book challenges readers to own their part in any conflict. It encourages readers to think about conflict in a very different way—not as something to be avoided at all costs, but rather as an integral part of the human condition that provides each of us with a challenge. That challenge is whether we want to grow.

As a lawyer I have been trained to think through all the possible arguments around any given problem. I often say how important it is to know, and understand, the opposing "strongest position" so I understand the weaknesses in mine. This orientation is about me; it is about winning; about being right. Sam challenges readers to engage in conflict differently: by listening and being open to being influenced. To me that was a game-changing concept—that I might actually listen differently, not just so I could plan what to say next to get my point across, but rather to truly understand a different point of view and be willing to change mine.

Positively Conflicted provides readers with insight. Sam does this through reflecting on his life and encouraging readers to do the same. He introduces readers to people he has encountered on his journey and shares their wisdom. I hope your conversation with Sam in reading *Positively Conflicted* awakens in you, as it has in me, a different way of approaching and learning from conflict.

Finally, in the book Sam tells readers about his hiatus from law school—when he impetuously dropped out and headed west. What he doesn't tell you is that one of the calls he made was to me and my then-fiancé to let us know he'd dropped out and wouldn't be able to stand up for us at our May 15 wedding. Now that I think about it, I guess Sam and I have been positively conflicted for a long time.

Holiday McKiernan
Executive Vice President, COO, and General Counsel
Lumina Foundation

Acknowledgments

Writing a book was never my goal. By thanking anyone, I will necessarily leave someone out.

Patty's commitment and love is at the core of everything that made this book possible.

The book began over a cup of coffee with Tim Orbaugh in Tucson four years ago. He invited Jane Wilson and Jason Orbaugh into the process, and they volunteered countless hours of encouragement, criticism, and opportunities. I could not be more grateful.

Just when I was ready to quit, Brad Gillum and Wendi Williams stepped in to keep the book alive.

My daughters and sons-in-law, Rachel, Grace, Mary, Ben, Chad, and Jess, kindly allowed me to include stories about them. My mom, dad, Kirk, and Joe bounced ideas back at me and asked about the book even if they might not have been interested.

Holly McKiernan so generously agreed to read the manuscript and write a foreword. Bonnie Gibson and Alan Blankstein also read the manuscript and bigheartedly went on the record to comment. Bill Henderson offered insight and guidance.

Bob Whitaker and many other friends and family let me talk

endlessly about a process that seemed to them and to me as if it would never end.

Tory Puntarelli, Greg Lloyd, Brad Surian, Jim Wahlen, and Mike Baye listened without complaint.

Joe Lee helped illustrate the cover, but more importantly supported the effort.

Doug Duncan encouraged me to write this book twenty-five years ago.

My law partners and legal assistants gave me the freedom to think and write while also practicing law full time. Without their generosity and patience, this book would be nothing more than empty ideas swimming in my head.

The Dignitaries Sympathy Group, where there are no dignitaries and there is no sympathy, told me to continue when I didn't want to.

Julie and Scott Stevens, the cousins, and Dave and Sally for years of love, support, and tolerance.

Melissa, Meagan, Gail, Angie, Rick, Tim, and both Joels for your prayers.

John, Al, and Jim for your friendship.

Patti, Chuck, and Winfield for your gentle feedback.

Dave Theil and Andy Karozos, my friends since childhood, helped these ideas germinate for more than fifty years.

Susan Wenger and Karen Thomas edited the book in a candid but kind way that made it infinitely better than it could have ever been without their talents and commitment.

Introduction

Brian was standing in the doorway of my office. We are equal partners in our law firm but twenty years apart in age. We were struggling to find the best way to handle cases and allocate fees. I felt the knot in my stomach growing as it became clear that we both wanted to be fair, but we had different thoughts on what that looked like. We are trial lawyers, so we understand how to advocate, convince, and rebut; however, those skills were getting us nowhere. I was starting to shut down, and Brian recognized my avoidance.

"For someone who makes his living helping people deal with their conflicts," Brian said, "you aren't very good at dealing with your own."

He was right, and he was not the first to make that observation. We are all imperfect, and our imperfections are amplified when we interact with others, especially when those interactions involve conflict. Our reactions to conflict usually involve a toxic mix of avoidance, denial, anger, embarrassment, shame, blame, resentment, excuses, and false bravado, frequently fueled by our sense of justice and a grasp for power. It's not pretty.

As my law partner said, I make a living dealing with conflict. I'm also a human being, so like all of us, I deal with conflict in daily life. For me, part of that experience has been recovering from alcoholism. I stopped drinking and began mediating at nearly the same time. Much of what I have discovered and applied in engaging conflict has arisen from mediating more than four thousand cases over the last twenty-five years, and also from being married, rearing children, and making commitments to myself or others that I've sometimes failed to keep. I have needed help. This book is my look at what has worked and not worked in my personal life and in my professional life as a mediator.

So what exactly are we talking about when we talk about conflict? Conflict arises whenever opposing forces or desires collide and cannot be readily reconciled. Phrases that come to mind when many of us think of conflict include fighting, yelling, choosing sides, aggression, antagonism, confrontation, battling, and warring. And, probably, most of us think of the goal of conflict as "winner takes all." Though conflict *can* be all those things, most often it is more nuanced and less binary.

Another way to describe our relationship to conflict is fear of losing what we have or of not getting what we want. Defined this way, conflict is not simply a battle between good and bad or right and wrong, with winners and losers. By rinsing our definition of negative and combative values and framing it more objectively, we can learn to approach the opposing forces in ourselves and with other people or circumstances with less righteousness, judgment, and blame and more compassion, insight, and equanimity.

But why engage conflict at all? Because conflict is an unavoidable part of being human. There will almost always be times when we fear losing something we have or not getting something we want. And even when we try to hide from conflict or deny that it's happening at all, it still affects us. Our attempts at avoidance and denial themselves create conflict. So whether we like it or not— and most of us don't—a life without conflict is fiction.

What makes conflict as a concept difficult to wrap our minds around is that it is fluid and changeable and often equivocal. It is not just a thing, a discrete event with defined boundaries and clear starting and stopping points. It is a happening, an interaction, a dynamic relationship between opposing forces and desires that we experience both internally and externally.

Internally, we can experience conflict when we press the snooze button on our alarm on a cold winter morning. The conflict is between the incompatible desires of wanting the immediate comfort of staying in bed *and* wanting to get to work on time. We cannot have both—what I call option F for fantasy. We experience external conflict when our coworkers reschedule a meeting with us, which forces us to rearrange our entire workday. The conflict is between their desire to meet at a time that works for them and our desire not to be inconvenienced by the change.

Conflict has many expressions. It can look like the self-hatred we feel when we choose to lie on the couch eating chips instead of meeting friends to exercise. It can feel like the fear of the vindictive boss who holds our future in her hands. Or the angry response to a teenager who breaks curfew once again. Perhaps it's the anxiety of confronting a lover when we are stuck and cannot imagine things ever changing. Or the feeling of defeat after doing what is right only to have it turn out all wrong. Though the experience of conflict elicits uncomfortable feelings, the fact that conflict exists is not something to feel bad about. Conflict just is.

But conflict does *feel* bad. The common theme of all conflicts is that they hurt. Whether they are excruciatingly painful or mildly irritating, we feel pain or discomfort anytime we experience incompatible desires. Which is why learning to accept or even embrace the discomfort of conflict is essential to engaging conflict positively. So is understanding the sources of conflict, including the ways we experience opposing forces within ourselves, like the struggle between sleeping in and getting to work on time; the way we experience opposing forces between ourselves and others, such as competing workplace agendas; and the way we experience opposing forces between ourselves and what life throws at us, like bad weather or institutional systems that inhibit our travel plans or life choices. Learning about the sparks that ignite conflict and the fuel that keeps it burning, the sources and drivers of conflict, will help us to identify conflict when it's happening. We may not be able to extinguish the spark before it ignites, but we can put out some of those fires before they blaze out of control. We want to understand where conflicts emerge and how they intensify—not so we can "manage" or sidestep conflict, but so we can engage conflict constructively and positively. Sometimes avoiding conflict *is* the best option, and we'll learn how to make that call. More often, however, conflict can only be delayed, not entirely avoided. Which means that engaging conflict is necessary and inescapable.

So let's make engaging conflict meaningful and expansive. Let's learn how to do conflict better.

Doing conflict better does not mean winning. This is not a book for those who see conflict as an enemy to be defeated, whether the conflict is within ourselves or with someone else. Nor is this a book for those who want foolproof steps for conflict engagement that work in all circumstances. Our emotions, relationships, and circumstances are too fluid to allow for immutable, unilateral, one-size-fits-all solutions. If you want to learn how to manipulate relationships to "get closure," you will need to look elsewhere. If you want the five steps, or ten steps, or perfect formula to get the results you want, you won't find that in this book.

This book is for the person who wants improved relationships that don't require the other person to do all the changing. The person who is ready for some deep introspection without being self-absorbed. The person who understands that complex problems are rarely amenable to a single simple solution. The person who wants to risk the vulnerability of stepping into the unknown to give engagement their best shot without expecting a guaranteed result. The person who is able to laugh at themselves to be part of something rather than excluded from it. The person who knows that courage emerges in the presence of fear, not in the absence of it.

Engaging positively with conflict will require a willingness to ask ourselves tough questions and reconsider whether being right is as important as we think. It will require exploring counterintuitive approaches, like courageously embracing discomfort, radically listening to others, and thoughtfully, if awkwardly, trying new methods. You will not learn to eliminate conflict from your life. You will learn to do it better.

Since I stopped drinking and began mediating in 1995, I have worked with thousands of people experiencing dramatically different circumstances. I have taught hundreds of law students, who now practice negotiation and conflict resolution around the world. I've included stories of my own conflicts and those of others. However, I have changed details, names, and identifiers to protect the confidentiality and privacy of people who have trusted me to help them. Information that is public record or for which I have received permission has not been changed. The lessons from my life and my own personal failures are real.

My wife, Patty, and I have been married for almost four decades. The stories that include Patty are true and told with her permission. These are accounts of hard lessons, failure, and humiliation, but they are also stories of insight, generosity, kindness, love, and grace. Conflicting emotions swim together.

You will read about some serious missteps on my part. I have hurt people. The quote on our mirror reads, "If you can't be a good example, you'll just have to be a horrible warning." I have been both. I am sharing lessons I learned from people who have been generous enough to help me without regard for whether I deserved it. Generosity in the face of conflict saved my life.

After Brian called me out on my own avoidance of conflict, we sat down and did the hard work of embracing the disagreement as an opportunity to have a serious conversation. There were times we were both heated, as we struggled not to convince the other person of our own definition of what was fair. We talked about time, tenure, expectations, contributions, benchmarks, values, and priorities. Each one of these factors influenced how we measured fairness differently, and we searched for a place to land on some common ground. Fundamentally, we liked and respected each other, and being clear about trust allowed us to have a candid, if sometimes uncomfortable, discussion. We reached an agreement on how to allocate cases and divide fees that accounted for some of the things we learned from listening to each other. Even though we reached an agreement, internalizing the agreement rather than focusing on the disagreement took time. Sometimes making the decision is harder than living with it, but neither is easy. We get to own our choices.

I am not offering legal advice or therapy to diagnose or fix you. However, you can improve your life if you engage conflict better. You can learn to recognize conflict, evaluate it, and make a choice as to whether the best decision is to engage it, set it aside for now, or abandon it altogether. You can learn to try new approaches on for size and see which ones fit you and which ones don't. You can learn to accept that you are one among many who fail and still succeed, who suffer and do not give up, who offer compassion when under attack.

I hope that you will find my stories relatable, my insight helpful, and my advice actionable.

1

The Storm Inside

As we discussed in the introduction, conflict arises whenever opposing forces or desires collide and cannot be readily reconciled. When opposing forces exist inside ourselves, we have internal conflict. For example, the desire for emotional intimacy can compete with the desire for emotional safety, leaving us conflicted about how to get close to someone without getting hurt. When our interests compete with someone else's interests, we have external conflict. An example might be the desire to advance professionally competing with a company's desire to limit promotions, placing our career goals in conflict with management's desire to maintain the status quo. Often, internal conflicts give rise to external conflicts. I might want to be successful in my career and also be afraid to fail (internal conflict). To avoid the risk of failure, I put forth the least amount of effort at work, which results in my being denied the promotion I want (external conflict).

Internal conflict (how we get in our own way of what we want or need) almost always arises from the fear of losing any of these four things: (1) survival/security, (2) affection/esteem, (3) power/

control, and (4) comfort/ease.¹ Survival and security can be translated into fear of death, injury, and financial insecurity. Esteem and affection convert to fear of shame, embarrassment, and social isolation. Power and control become the fear of uncertainty and the unknown, powerlessness, and loss of mobility. Comfort and ease encompass fear of unpleasantness, pain, and constraints on our choices and freedoms. The fears often overlap.

An internal conflict can be as basic as the opposing forces of wanting to lose weight and also wanting to eat chocolate cake after every meal. We *want* to fit into our favorite pair of jeans, but we're *afraid* of losing the comfort we derive from eating our favorite dessert, so we continue to eat cake despite the negative emotions that come with not pursuing what we really value. Boom—we're in the midst of a conflict. To top it off, we then add another layer of conflict by not sticking to our goals, which results in the loss of self-esteem and feelings of shame or embarrassment. The equation is simple to understand, but experiencing it is not. Most of us prefer the fantasy option of eating the cake *and* fitting into the jeans.

Internal conflicts can have graver consequences than just not fitting into our old jeans. Let's say you overhear your boss using hateful and discriminatory language when describing a coworker. Do you call your boss out, quietly pay a visit to HR and hope action will be taken, or stay silent? You want to live by your values, which reject bigotry, but you fear the pain that comes with losing financial security, which you risk by speaking up. You are faced with the competing forces of staying employed (survival) or standing up for your friend (connection with your group) and standing up for your principles (esteem, for yourself and from your coworkers and

---

1   Cynthia Bourgeault, *Centering Prayer and Inner Awakening* (Lanham, MD: Cowley Publications, 2004), 147. Bourgeault does not identify these as fears but as desires to let go of in a meditative practice. She addresses the first three, and I've added the last one, "comfort and ease."

friends). One common life situation can trigger multiple fears and complex internal and external conflict.

Back to the chocolate cake versus ideal weight dilemma. What if the weight issue is more than aesthetic? Perhaps the excess weight is causing serious health problems. And what if those problems not only affect you but also those close to you? Your friends and family want you around for a long time. They also might want to hike on summer vacations with you, or they might rely on you for the family's well-being. Again, a single circumstance can trigger all four fears (survival, social isolation, loss of mobility, and pain).

Conflict Hurts

We know we're experiencing internal conflict when we feel discomfort or pain. The fact that we all experience discomfort and pain at various times is evidence that we all experience internal conflict. It's unavoidable. But many of us bury our heads in the sand and pretend things are fine. Some of us self-medicate, and most of us engage in other numbing or distracting behaviors to avoid the discomfort of conflict. To paraphrase sociobiologist Robert Trivers, our consciousness evolved to fool ourselves so that we could better fool others.[2] I'd add that we also unconsciously fool ourselves so that we avoid feeling bad. But by putting off the inevitable, we fail to acknowledge that the inevitable is still going to happen.

We're going to look at ways to stop fooling ourselves, but first it's important to understand the effect internal conflict has on our well-being—physically, emotionally, and relationally. The following are some of the negative impacts of ignoring our inner conflicts:

> » *Conflict takes up room in our minds.* We have finite energy to devote to our daily tasks, and struggling with an internal

---

2   Robert Trivers, *Deceit and Self-Deception: Fooling Yourself the Better to Fool Others* (London: Allen Lane, 2011).

conflict means there is less time, energy, and attention for other things. We may be working harder than ever when we're struggling to avoid dealing with an internal conflict, but we can still appear sloppy, lazy, or uncommitted to those around us.

» *Conflict compromises our health.* The psychological contortions we perform to avoid the pain that accompanies internal conflict puts enormous strain on our emotional and physical health. Anxiety, poor sleep, substance abuse, weight fluctuations, and myriad physiological stress result from or are exacerbated by our attempts to ignore inner struggles.

» *Conflict may be hurting others.* We might think only we suffer from our internal conflicts, but chances are the people we're surrounded by see some manifestation of our struggle and feel it, too. Family members, friends, coworkers, and the clerk at the convenience store are often casualties in our battle with ourselves.

Get Your Priorities Straight

While we all experience internal conflict, it doesn't have to have catastrophic consequences on our relationships, our careers, or ourselves. So how can we tend to the turmoil inside our minds? First, we want to see if our priorities align with our behaviors.

The first time I began to understand that some of the problems in my life originated within me, I was thirty-seven years old and trapped in a car with an insightful, strong-willed, sixty-seven-year-old man named Red. Red helped me to own up to my role in the storm that was raging inside me.

I was at the nadir of my struggles with addiction. It was 1995, and I was drinking about a quart of vodka a day. I was failing in my duties as a husband, father, and practicing lawyer. It was the darkest part of my personal and professional history, and the only tool I had for dealing with the fallout of my internal conflicts was to deflect responsibility and blame onto others. I was dying physically, emotionally, and spiritually, and I was completely unaware of it.

Each morning during that period, I awakened with an excruciating hangover and little memory of the night before. I would ask my wife subtle questions to piece together the previous evening without letting on that I didn't remember any of it. I frequently learned that I had hurt or embarrassed myself or others. After I had the story, I spent much of the rest of the day avoiding, denying, and drinking to forget it. Eventually, I spent more time drinking and hiding than working or engaging with my family.

Although I didn't know it then, January 29, 1995, was the day I took my last drink. I also didn't know that it was the day I began to stop blaming others for my problems.

In an uncharacteristically honest moment, I had shared my struggles with alcohol dependence with a client who was in recovery. This client unwittingly helped save my marriage, my career, and, likely, my life: he introduced me to Red, someone he thought could help me get sober.

Red lived up to his name, with thick, gray-streaked auburn hair and matching beard. At six foot two and well over two hundred pounds, he was a force. His commanding presence was aided by a deep baritone voice, which was most often raised to a near shout. The fact that he was pushing seventy did nothing to diminish his authority or energy. He was imposing, wise, and passionately relentless.

Shortly after we met, Red informed me he was heading up to Adrian, Michigan, the following Saturday and added, "You're coming with me." It was not a request. And though I was not accustomed to people ordering me around, I couldn't find the fortitude to protest, despite that it meant a five-hour drive in a car with a terrifying man I barely knew, and drinking was not an option. So that Saturday I found myself strapped into the passenger seat of a white Crown Vic, which reminded me uncomfortably of a police cruiser. As Red headed north, I began looking for a way to escape, wondering how much it would hurt if I jumped out of the moving car with a tuck and roll.

We hadn't even made it across the county line when Red started in. "I bet your head is spinning. You have no idea what you've gotten yourself into, taking this trip with me." That was an understatement. I waited a moment for him to clue me in, but instead, he carried on. "Do you love your wife? Your kids? Your job?" He didn't pause for an answer, so I sat there with my mouth hanging open while he responded for me. "Of course you do. But not one thing about your behavior suggests that. You can't be honest with yourself, so how can you be honest with anyone else?"

I wanted to argue. Wanted to tell him he had no right to speak to me that way. That he hardly knew me and couldn't know the kind of man I was. I wanted to call him a long string of increasingly insulting names. Instead, I stayed silent and watched the trees flash by as we sped along a flat expanse of I-69 through northern Indiana.

Red's monologue went on for what felt like hours. The drone of his voice eventually turned into white noise as I wished for a collision, a flood, an alien abduction—anything that might bring an end to this interminable ride. Numb, painfully sober, and wondering what god I had angered, I was relieved when we finally stopped for lunch at a diner outside Fort Wayne.

The interior of the restaurant was aggressively green and dotted with ancient Formica tables. The fluorescent lights made the white aprons worn by the servers glow. And the place smelled like someone had dunked Thanksgiving dinner into a deep fat fryer.

We slid into a booth, and before I could pick up a menu, Red was ordering for both of us. "Two grilled pork sandwiches, home-fried potatoes, and green beans for here… and two chocolate shakes to go," he told our server.

Before the food arrived, Red picked up where he'd left off on the drive. And with nothing else to do, I listened.

"You imagine yourself a success, don't you? All the bad stuff in your life, that's the result of circumstance, or is someone else's fault." That part wasn't a question. He pointed a thick, calloused finger at me, and I tried not to flinch under his scrutiny. "If you're such a success and your way is working, why are you sitting here in this restaurant with some old man you barely know?"

I'd been wondering the same thing for the last two hundred miles.

Red put his arms on the table and leaned toward me. "Kid, you're a mess. If you want to get better, I can help."

I froze. I could protest if I really wanted to. Tell him he was out of line, that he had no right. Hell, I could call a cab and be back home in time for dinner and pretend this strange fugue-state nightmare had never happened. Instead, I did something really out of character: I agreed with him. I *was* a mess, and there was no denying it. I didn't know if I believed that he could help me, but I suddenly realized that I wanted to hear him out. After all, how was my way working? Not everyone is driven by addiction issues, but many people describe similar feelings when repeatedly confronted with conflict in their lives.

Red seemed to take my silence for acquiescence. He leaned back in, grabbed a paper napkin, and flagged down the server to borrow a pen. He wrote down five words and slid the napkin toward me.

"Everything in life—I mean, everything—falls into one of these categories," he said.

I saw the following list written in a heavy black scrawl:

Recreation
Belief System
Health/Wellness
Work/School
Family/Social

"There's nothing in life that can't be placed into one of these categories." He said with great confidence, loud enough for the whole restaurant to hear. As I shrunk away from the stares of the other patrons, Red leaned in closer. "Here's what I want you to do."

At this point, I want to invite you to do the short exercise, and we will discuss it when you are done.

Red's Exercise

The activity Red gave me to complete was eye-opening. I'll offer some working definitions of the five categories, but feel free to define them in a way that is most meaningful for you. After you have read the definitions, you can do the exercise on the graph.

Recreation

Where you find respite from the rigors of your daily grind. It could include reading, exercising, sports, listening to music, having coffee with friends, or going out to dinner. Are your recreational activities a priority or an afterthought?

Belief System

The umbrella or operating system under which we live our lives. It can be a meditation practice, religious practice, political or world view, or ethical creed that involves feelings about fairness, justice, balance, authority, humility, forgiveness, resentment, and pride. How carefully and consciously do you integrate your belief system into your daily life?

Health/Wellness

The ways you value your mental and physical well-being, such as meeting regularly with a trusted friend, therapist, or wellness practitioner; maintaining a daily workout schedule or going on a daily walk; and eating healthfully. Do you have practices that support your emotional and physical health? How important are your practices in relation to these other priorities?

Work/School

The activities and tasks that drive our daily routine, whether we are students, dockworkers, accountants, or stay-at-home parents. Work is not necessarily something that pays a wage. It is often what we "have" to do. This category usually changes as we age, as our families increase or decrease, and as our vocations evolve. How intentional are you about what you "have" to do?

Family/Social

The importance we place on interpersonal relationships. How we define family and the way we value social interaction are different for everyone. Introverts may practice activities related to this category differently from extroverts while still prioritizing it at the same level. How much effort do you put into your relationships?

	Recreation	
	Belief system	
	Health/wellness	
	Work/school	
	Family/social	

To begin, on the left side of the chart above, rank your priorities from 1 to 5 (1 being your highest priority). This is not an exercise for you to judge yourself. Just be as honest as you can about your ideal hierarchy of the categories. Don't take too long and go with your gut.

After you've ranked your categories and entered them on the chart, imagine someone following you around for a couple of days with a video camera. In the right-hand column of the chart, rank the categories according to what you believe the video evidence would reveal are your priorities

Do the two columns of ranking match?

For the overwhelming number of people who do this exercise, the numbers on the left do not match the numbers on the right. If your numbers don't match, then you and I have that in common. As it turns out, we are in a very big internal-conflict club made up of nearly everyone who does the exercise.

If your numbers do not match, it might be worth considering how you can bring them into alignment. Talk to someone you trust to be honest with you, and ask what they think your priorities are. Show them the chart without your numbers, and ask them to rank your priorities as they see them. If they observe discrepancies, perhaps they would be willing to share with you places where they think you might be getting in your own way or places where your perceptions might not be as clear as you believe them to be.

Now back to my own conversations with Red. Sitting in the diner, I completed the same exercise I just asked you to do.

Unsurprisingly, my numbers did not match up.

Then Red got to the crux of the issue. He wadded up the napkin, leaned in close, and lowered his voice. This time, I was hanging on his every word.

"Sam," he said, almost kindly, "every conflict begins with you. There is the person you claim to be and the person your behavior shows you to be. You probably don't even realize the way that disparity affects you and the people around you. You feel fear, stress, anger, and anxiety, but you don't know why. You can't acknowledge your internal conflict, so you lie to yourself and others. Until you are aware of this, you cannot have honest relationships with yourself or other people." Red paused and looked at me.

"OK," I said, not wanting to invite an argument, "let's say you're right. What next?"

"There are only two ways to resolve internal conflicts," Red said. "One, you can change your behavior to match your priorities. Two, you can change your priorities to match your behavior. There are no other options for resolution."

We left the restaurant with our chocolate shakes and headed north.

Conflict Integration

That drive with Red happened many years ago. I continued to be a litigator and mediator but stopped drinking. Red offered up a mirror that reflected that my drinking was a symptom of being too afraid to live life on life's terms. He promised help to go through life without an anesthetic. I was ready. Red and I maintained our friendship until he died, twenty-one years later. Throughout that time, he continued to challenge me to face my internal conflicts—honestly, openly, and courageously.

The solution Red offered, while illuminating, was incomplete. Whereas he believed there are only two ways of resolving internal conflicts—changing priorities or changing behaviors—my experience, personally and professionally, has been that despite our best efforts to align our priorities with our behavior, most people continue to struggle with internal conflicts. I've asked thousands of people to do this exercise, and I can count on one hand the number of people who say that all their priorities match their behaviors.

Red's solution was logically correct, but there was something too tidy about it. You see, *resolution* suggests a definable end to a conflict. If we measure success only by permanent resolutions, we set the bar impossibly high, often lying to ourselves and others because we want so desperately to wrap up our conflict and move on. Over the years, I have found actual resolution to be far more dynamic and nuanced. In reality, some conflicts are simply beyond resolution. When I stopped drinking, my battle with alcoholism didn't end. My relationship issues were not magically fixed. For most of us, the day never arrives when we are scrubbed clean of our internal conflicts. We do not always resolve our internal conflicts, and if we do, the resolution may be temporary.

The objective, then, is not that we resolve every internal conflict, because often, we won't. Rather, the aim is to develop awareness about our conflicts and consciously respond to the constant oscillation between the alignment and misalignment of our priorities and behaviors. This is our eternal dance with internal conflict. What I call *conflict integration*. By practicing awareness of our internal conflicts, understanding their significance, and thoughtfully responding to the dissonance between our priorities and our behaviors, we can integrate what we want with what we fear losing (what we need) to achieve wholeness and meaning in our lives. Though we continue to attempt to resolve our internal conflicts, resolution itself is sometimes a by-product of awareness and acceptance of the role internal conflict plays in our lives.

My dad was a good example of someone who managed conflict integration. He was the youngest of five children and grew up during the Great Depression. His family went from living as successful farmers to losing nearly everything. The family was able to stay in their home because of two aunts who had enough money to keep the family sheltered and fed. They ate by curing cabbage into sauerkraut and butchering pigs in their backyard. At the beginning of each summer, my dad put on a straw hat and a pair of overalls and picked potato bugs for a penny a bug.

My dad was scheduled to be drafted after he graduated from high school in 1943, so he enlisted in what was then the Army Air Corps, to have a choice of the branch of the military in which he would serve. He served as a radio man for aircraft flying in China and India.

When World War II ended, the GI Bill allowed him to go to college, which would have been unimaginable for him before the war. He became a pharmacist and retired at sixty-four years of age, still married to my mom and with my brother and me grown and on our own.

For more than thirty years, my dad worked in pharmacies owned by other people. He started with a small independent pharmacy and continued on at increasingly larger pharmacies as they

bought the smaller ones. As the pharmacies got bigger, his opportunities to connect with the people he served, which had been his
favorite part of the job, diminished. He did not like the last twenty
years of his job, yet he worked six or seven days a week for more
than thirty years. He did it without complaint.

His life experience had been that all security could be lost in an
instant. He experienced that in the Depression. He experienced it
again when he lost young friends in World War II. He did not prefer the control that larger corporations had over his work situation,
but he was afraid of losing the security of a steady job. At the same
time, he was afraid of doing his job in a way that did not always
serve the customers as he thought was best. He also feared risking
the failure and embarrassment that could come with opening his
own business, something he sometimes regretted not attempting.
These were my father's constantly competing interests and fears,
his internal conflicts.

He integrated his internal conflict by not allowing himself to
be completely controlled by his dissatisfaction with a job that required working sixty hours a week under conditions he didn't like.
He focused on what he enjoyed: spending time with my mother, bowling and drinking beer with his buddies, and teaching my
brother and me how to field ground balls and change tires. He never talked about the war or disliking his job until much later, and
then only a little. If my dad had not integrated his dislike for his
job with the need to keep his job, he could have become resentful
of his responsibilities, including his kids; he could have strained his
relationship with my mother; and he might not have found enjoyment and satisfaction outside of work.

My dad never did Red's exercise, rating his five priorities in life
and thinking about what a video camera might reveal about them,
but he accepted and integrated things he preferred and things he
didn't. In a moment of reflection before he died at ninety-four, he
told me, "Your mom and I did not have a lot of money when we
retired, but we had a lot of fun, and those years between sixty-four

and eighty-four were among the happiest of my life." I know my mom agreed.

Different Smokes for Different Folks

Our lives require us to deal with competing interests that can't always be easily reconciled, and all of us are doing conflict integration daily, sometimes consciously and sometimes not. Perhaps we cannot fix every conflict, but we can learn to live better with conflicts and not give as much headspace to the four categories of things we fear losing. The following is an example of two people with the same internal conflict who ultimately chose to integrate it differently.

Sherry and Walt are smokers. They both had tried quitting in all sorts of ways but had always returned to it. They are bright, have jobs and families, and generally enjoy their lives. They also deeply enjoy smoking. Even thinking about their next cigarette at a break brings them pleasure. They are well aware of the research about the negative effects that smoking has on health, so they have fears surrounding survival. They also have fears around loss of social connection, because they know some people see smoking as a personal weakness, and around loss of comfort and ease, because smoking gives them a lot of enjoyment, and stopping would cause some discomfort.

Sherry and Walt have a friend in common, Christy, who is not a smoker. Christy does not care if Sherry and Walt smoke other than that they are both friends of hers. The three of them had the following conversation.

"I love to smoke, but I hate the financial cost, the way people think about me, and the fact that it could kill me," Sherry said.

"I'm embarrassed, but I love it too. When I go to my kids' ballgames, I'm either inside jonesing for a cigarette or outside missing the game," Walt said.

"It seems to me," Christy said, "that you are damned if you do and damned if you don't. You are struggling to make a decision, and either choice comes with pain. There is no easy option, and you are just beating yourselves up by not choosing one. When you smoke, you don't fully enjoy it because you think about what you are missing and you feel bad that you can't quit. When you stop smoking, you have a hard time enjoying anything because you are addicted to the cigarettes and it is physically and emotionally painful to not smoke. There is not a pain-free option."

Sherry and Walt nodded in unison.

"My suggestion," Christy said, "is either to commit to smoking and enjoy it and stop shaming yourselves with failed efforts to stop, or to enlist all the help you need to make stopping your top priority over everything else. As it is now, you aren't getting the full enjoyment of smoking or the full enjoyment of quitting."

Sherry decided to keep smoking and to practice not feeling bad about it. And it did take practice to let go of the guilt. Walt stopped all his extracurricular activities with his family for a while and enrolled in an intensive outpatient program to quit. He stopped smoking but still wonders whether he made the best decision when he sees Sherry smoke.

The fears of losing security, connection, and comfort all danced in Sherry's and Walt's heads without their permission and sometimes without their awareness. Once Christy pointed out that the conflict arising from their lack of commitment to either choice was sucking the joy out of the habit, Walt and Sherry made decisions that integrated their internal opposing forces. Sherry chose to continue smoking, with full knowledge of the risks. She no longer feels embarrassed about smoking because she owns it. Walt chose to stop smoking, with full knowledge that he would miss the pleasure of it. He does not have to feel disconnected from his family, though he owns missing having a cigarette.

Conflict integration begins with acknowledging competing interests and maybe even that one choice *should be* better than another. It continues by making a decision and living with it, knowing that there will be some discomfort with either choice, but also some satisfaction and adventure as well.

Takeaway

There are times when alignment of our priorities and behaviors happens, and we can celebrate it, if only quietly in our own minds. But none of us live our lives in consistent alignment with the idealized version that we have in our heads or write down on paper. Having some compassion for ourselves and others when we fall short opens a window to connect with rather than push away from others. It also allows us not to live in shame of our shortcomings.

Action

When you berate yourself for what you see as a failure to keep a commitment to yourself or to live your "best life" (to use a phrase I strongly dislike), take a moment to remember that you are in a big club of folks who get up and do their best but often do not measure up. This can actually connect you to people rather than make you feel ashamed to be among them.

2

You Versus the World

We've all heard the saying "pick your battles." But when our interests come into opposition with someone else's or when someone pits their agenda against ours, the stakes feel too high to cede any ground. We stand on principle (our own) to defend what we have or demand what we want. Hello, external conflict! As we discussed in the previous chapter, external conflicts often arise from our own internal conflicts, and they always arise from the fears surrounding our security, social connection, power, and comfort.

External conflicts emerge in every type of relationship—between family members, business partners, and nations. Decisions about how aging parents should be cared for, money should be divided, and international disputes should be handled can all lead to conflict. External conflict ends marriages, dissolves businesses, and starts wars.

But it doesn't have to. When we stop running from fear and stop blaming others, we might find a positive path through the conflict without leaving ourselves and others standing in piles of personal rubble. Outcomes of external conflicts are always uncertain, and resolutions are not guaranteed, so uneasiness is ever present, but new possibilities emerge when we choose to step into the conflict, listen compassionately to the other person, and acknowledge our own role in the disagreement.

The World Keeps Spinning … Just Not Around You

The pain we encounter in external conflict often stems from the belief that our circumstances are more meaningful than other people's. That doesn't make us all narcissists by any means. The only experiences we can fully internalize are our own, so we are naturally more concerned with them and influenced by them. I witnessed an example of our tendency toward self-focus play out when I overheard a conversation between two friends recently.

"I saw the doctor about my headaches, and the tests confirmed that I have brain cancer," Howie said.

"I'm sorry," his friend, Kent, responded, just short of dismissively. "I just found out I have to replace the foundation on my house."

"Did you hear what I just said?"

"I did," Kent answered. "I was just too wrapped up in my own bad day."

These were two friends, and one had a life-threatening medical diagnosis. The other had a financially difficult life circumstance. It's not that Kent didn't care about Howie. He was just too caught up in his own financial scare to immediately process the devastating news that Howie had just received. We do not do our best listening when our resilience is low and we're scared.

Howie and Kent are still friends, but this short exchange illustrates how our natural self-centeredness can lower our capacity to listen compassionately and can create conflict when there was none to be found.

This focus on self can help us survive in a hostile environment, but it is self-defeating in a collaborative environment, which should be the goal of most healthy families and workplaces.

When we consider ourselves and our circumstances unique and supremely important, we put our own needs first and think we're entitled to feel better, all the time. This way of thinking inevitably results in behavior that is dismissive of the needs of others and leads to many conflicts with spouses, partners, colleagues, and friends. If we cannot move beyond self-absorption, those conflicts usually end badly.

Consider this simplistic breakdown of how self-absorption can land us into conflict with others. I have a friend, Tom, who is a great guy. Besides being a great guy, Tom is also routinely late. Because Tom considers himself a great guy, being late does not bother him much.

Tom is supposed to be at his office by 8:00 every weekday morning, but he usually leaves his home just before 8:00—too late to arrive at work on time. He thinks, "I'm not late *yet*." Once the clock ticks to 8:01 a.m. (with ten minutes left in his commute), he starts thinking of reasons that justify his tardiness.

Tom's unwillingness (he would call it *inability*) to be on time isn't just a result of poor planning. It stems from his belief that his circumstances justify his lateness, and that his situation is unique and thereby more important or meaningful than the situations of others, although he would not put it this way. None of this makes Tom a terrible person, but it does put him at odds with numerous people in his life, including his boss, coworkers, and family members, who know they have to plan around his perpetual tardiness. Or exclude Tom from activities, or fire him. By failing to make more thoughtful decisions about how his behavior affects others, Tom forces everyone else to make trade-off decisions about him.

When we make excuses for failing to honor commitments, we communicate that our circumstances are more important than other people's. Behavior that consistently reveals our self-focus damages trust and creates barriers to productive engagement. It creates an environment of disrespect, which is particularly damaging when we are working through some kind of conflict. People who feel disrespected do not respond well to those who have disrespected them.

We all have made mistakes and failed to keep commitments—sometimes repeatedly. If I excuse behavior that conflicts internally with my own values or externally with others, I need to own it and stop apologizing. I need to change or accept the consequences. Among the consequences can be the unspoken resentment people in our lives feel toward us.

I Want You to *Want* to Do It . . .

Bright, honest, and well-meaning people disagree. The difficulty in resolving disagreements is that we consider ourselves bright, honest, and well-meaning and the people we're in disagreement with less bright, less honest, and less well-meaning . . . or much worse. It is not surprising that they feel the same way about us. We all think we have just the right amount of common sense, fairness, and morality . . . and they think the same about themselves. We all feel righteous, and when we experience the discomfort of disagreement, we believe the easiest solution is for the other person to change. And we don't stop there. We don't just want others to stop fighting with us and do our bidding, we want them to tell us we are right, to see the world our way—and to be happy about it.

In a 2006 movie called *The Break-Up*, Jennifer Aniston and Vince Vaughn play a romantically involved couple who live together. In one scene, after a party at their house, Aniston's character is cleaning up while Vaughn's character parks himself on the couch to watch TV. It becomes clear she's irritated with him for not helping, but when he gets up to help, she's still upset. He doesn't understand.

"You just said that you want me to help you do the dishes," he says with exasperation.

In a moment of clarity, she says, "I want you to *want* to do the dishes."[1]

Haven't we all felt this way? We get what we want, but it's not enough. It's only when we get it that we realize we wanted more. Because having someone surrender the fight is not enough—we want a wholesale change in the way they think. That is too big an ask.

My wife pointed out the risk of making such a big ask during a tense exchange many years into our marriage. It's important to note that those we live with offer the most opportunities to practice our conflict engagement skills. Patty and I were in our living room, arguing about something that was so inconsequential I can't remember the substance of it. It was fall, and I could see the changing leaves outside our living room window. Funny that I recall the surroundings and how I felt but not the substance of the argument. Though the details are lost to time, I remember that I was righteously invested in my point of view. As the argument became more heated, I leaned harder into my agenda. Listening was not on my radar as I made my point. In that moment nothing was more important than being right *and* having Patty acknowledge it.

At one point, Patty paused, put her hands on her hips, looked me in the eye, and said, "Would you rather be right, or would you rather be married?"

This seemed to be a trick question, and I did not answer. To me, we were arguing about the now forgotten topic. To Patty, it was not the topic but the attitude and the relationship that were in play. But her perspective was the furthest thing from my mind. It's embarrassing, but I can recall the context and how I felt at the time, but not how Patty looked until she asked me the question. My behavior was hardly the stuff of great conflict engagement or relationship care.

---

1   *The Break-Up*, directed by Peyton Reed (Universal Pictures, 2006).

Patty left the room before I could figure out what to say. Her question may have been rhetorical—of course I'd rather be married. But in my quest to be right and have her see that I was right, my priorities were upside down. My day job is conflict resolution; however, when put to the test in my own life, I don't always do so well.

When we invest deeply in our own rightness and the "injustice" of having someone else disagree, the bigger picture goes out of focus. In the first example, the Jennifer Aniston character got the behavior she wanted from Vince Vaughn's character but not the attitude she wanted. In the second example, Patty got neither the behavior nor the attitude. Patty challenged me to not lose sight of the forest for the trees—to get my priorities straight and value our relationship over my investment in being right.

Jennifer Aniston's character isn't wrong to want more—to want the attitude to match the behavior—but in wanting it so much, she failed to have any appreciation for what she did get. While she's right that the whole package of behavior and attitude is better than one or the other, we sometimes need to patiently wait to see if the behavior eventually morphs into the desired attitude. It may or may not, and then we have other decisions to make.

In the case of Patty and me, I was so focused on wanting Patty to agree I was right that I lost sight of the fact that our relationship was more important than any given disagreement. As with wanting the whole package of behavior and attitude, there isn't anything wrong with wanting to have a spirited debate. But a debate suggests some back-and-forth between the participants. There was no back-and-forth between Patty and me in this instance because I was demanding a specific response from Patty and ignoring what she thought. I was only willing to accept that she agree with me. I was blind to how my investment in being right was damaging my investment in the larger relationship. We should all remember: *being right is really expensive and way overrated.*

Owning Our Part

If you're feeling uncomfortable after reading some of the hard truths here, that's a good sign you're willing to consider some troubling facts. If you feel that you're in conflict with this book, then it might have value for you. Nearly everyone can benefit from understanding the ins and outs of external conflict: what drives it, what drives our responses to it, and how our reactions can escalate, diminish, or, sometimes, resolve it.

One challenge is that many of us don't want to admit that we are one of the drivers of any conflict we find ourselves in. We are always part of the problem. We discuss this in detail in chapter 10, "Accepting Responsibility," but for now it's important to recognize that our role in the conflict, however large or small, must be owned and addressed in order to have any hope of improving the situation. If we want to do conflict better, we need to direct our energy to our part in the conflict...but in a different way.

The challenge is to step out of our singular perspective and be aware that other people can experience the exact same event and perceive it, process it, and react to it differently. Before we try to talk them out of their perspective, we need to spend more time paying attention to how they see a situation and then challenge our own view of it. Sometimes the truth of another's perspective can be jarring, but hearing and accepting it is powerful.

In the last year I was drinking, Patty and I built a new home. Patty didn't really want to build a house or move. She was perfectly happy with the home where we lived with our three young daughters. Nevertheless, in a reluctant surrender to my relentless agenda, Patty agreed. Mostly she turned it over to me and tolerated my obsession.

When the house was completed and it came time to move, I had just stopped drinking. The community of people who were helping me stop drinking and live differently suggested that a new house was not a good idea. "One major change at a time is about all any of us can handle," my friend Jeremy told me. "You've just stopped drinking, and moving your family might not be the best choice."

Jeremey's suggestion that we not move would never have occurred to me. It was jarring, and initially I discounted it out of hand. The suggestion made no sense.

"How did you reach the decision to build a house?" Jeremy asked.

"Patty and I talked about it and she agreed," I said, leaving out the part where I badgered her for months.

"When I was drunk," Jeremy said, as if he knew there was more, "I was like a battering ram to get whatever I wanted. I beat people into emotional submission to get what I wanted, no matter the cost. Maybe that wasn't you, but you've told me that Patty didn't want to move, and yet you spent months of time and energy building a house with almost no participation from her."

"Maybe I was a little pushy," I said.

"My guess is that there are lots of things you've been 'a little pushy' about," Jeremy said. "Maybe it's time to own some of that."

I was uncomfortable with how clearly Jeremy saw through what I was leaving out as I told the story of how "we" decided to build a house. After some tossing and turning, I decided I was more afraid of drinking than of losing money on a house. We sold it without sleeping a night in it. Patty was relieved. Having a light shined on my role in a conflict and taking some concrete action to make amends for it was an early example of seeing that I have a role in any conflict in which I find myself.

House Epilogue

Internal conflicts can create external conflicts as we try to defend against the truth. We can sidestep many external conflicts by not becoming defensive about our personal struggles.

Our daughters were aware that we had built the house and

never moved in, but I don't remember many conversations with them about it. My summary, if someone asked, was to say, "We just changed our mind." That was the clean and simple version, and I assumed our girls saw it the same way, to the extent they thought of it at all.

Our youngest daughter, Mary, as I learned later, was quite capable of communicating the reason we didn't move in. She was about two years old when we built the house, and about ten when she and a friend were buckled into the back seat of our red Ford Taurus station wagon as I drove them home from a school choir practice.

"Can we drive by the house we built?" Mary asked.

This had become a frequent request from our girls.

"Sure," I agreed, not thinking much of it. I drove by the house, which was on the way we took to her friend's home.

"Why didn't you move?" Mary's friend Allison asked as we drove by.

"Because my dad's a drunk and my mom didn't want to," Mary answered without any particular emotion.

"Oh," Allison said, unaffected. They moved on to their next topic of conversation in the back seat.

I felt the hair stand up on the back of my neck. I was embarrassed, even though my recovery from alcoholism was not a secret in our community. Sometimes it is particularly enlightening to hear someone's perspective when they share it with someone else rather than directly with us. If you are in a conflict, listen carefully not only to what is being said to you but what is being said about you to others. And don't be surprised by your uncomfortable reaction to the truth.

There was no conflict in the exchange between the girls about the house we never lived in. Mary had done nothing but tell the truth with great efficiency. But a conflict could have developed had I challenged Mary on her recollection or told her to keep something secret. Sometimes the most instructive external conflicts are the ones we never have.

Roles and Expectations

External conflicts often arise when two people think differently about their roles in a relationship. The relationship can be ongoing and committed, such as that between a boss and an employee, a
parent and a child, or partners in a business or personal connection.
Conversely, the relationship can be more transient and distant,
such as that between a customer or client and a service worker or
provider. Since we have all been either parents or children, looking
at the parent-child relationship provides many examples of how
the ways we misinterpret the roles we play or expect others to play
can lead to conflict.

A school psychologist once described three stages of parenting—dictator, tour guide, and consultant. The dictator stage is when
a parent has virtually complete control. Usually a parent is a dictator from when their children are born to when they're about seven
or eight years old. When parents are dictators, they control pretty
much all of what their babies or young children do, including what
they eat, where they are, and whom they spend time with.

The tour-guide stage runs from when children are seven or
eight years old until they are sixteen or seventeen, depending on
the child and the parents. As a tour guide, parents put up guard-
rails, set schedules, and create penalties for broken rules, but they
cannot completely control what their children eat, where they are,
and whom they are with.

The final parenting stage is consultant. This runs from when
children are around seventeen or eighteen years old until the rest
of our lives. A consultant provides guidance when asked, but does
not give unsolicited advice.

After describing the three stages, my psychologist friend said
that the biggest conflicts between parents and children, grown or
not, occur when parents think the children are in one stage, and the
children think they are in a different stage. I have two examples

of this involving my oldest daughter, Rachel—one when she was young and one after she was a married adult with two boys of her own.

Expectations

Creating and enforcing chores for our daughters was not a parenting strength for Patty or me. Nevertheless, we sometimes set out to remedy that.

When Rachel was twelve, we decided she was old enough to cut the grass. Old enough and willing were two different things. When it was time to for her to do it, I told her, and she flat out refused. She yelled that she wouldn't and plopped herself down with her legs curled under her in an old blue recliner in our family room. I was *fuming* at her rebellion.

For a moment, I thought about picking her up, carrying her out to the lawn mower, and laying her down in the grass. It would have been a bad choice, and I didn't do it. Instead I tried to explain that we ask very little of her and she needed to go cut the grass…now! No change. As I approached the chair to make my point in a louder tone of voice, she bolted from the chair and stomped upstairs to her bedroom, all the while yelling at me. By now she was crying, and I was just plain mad. I stood there confused.

My plan was perfectly reasonable to me, and now it was going to hell in a handbasket in a way that surprised me. Rachel's response to cutting the grass seemed disproportionate to the ask from my perspective. But her response made complete sense to her. I could remember being twelve, but at forty-two, I had nothing more than my perception of being twelve that might or might not have been accurate. I do remember feeling pretty disconnected from my parents as I entered my teenaged years. Then it occurred to me that making my twelve-year-old cut the grass was not the most important thing in the world.

I quietly walked up the stairs to her bedroom and sat on the floor in the hallway outside her open door. She was on her bed, crying, and I said nothing. After a few minutes her crying became more of a whimper, and she moved to the floor. I continued to sit, not saying anything.

Slowly, she inched her way toward me and sat next to me on the floor in the hallway.

"I'm sorry," I said without further explanation. She gave me a hug and said nothing.

I don't remember how or whether the grass got cut.

This is a single moment in our lives, which Rachel may not recall. You may wonder what it has to do with conflict for adults. I'd say everything. We will probably have the most opportunities to engage with conflict in our homes. The things we learn there can be carried out to the streets and into our businesses.

I believed I was right in having chores for our twelve-year-old daughter. I also thought that in my role as tour guide, I had the authority to enforce rules. However, when I was frustrated and Rachel disagreed, I was tempted to go back to the role of dictator. It did not help. Only when I behaved differently from the way I felt—when I adjusted my role at the moment—and showed some compassion for a twelve-year-old in full meltdown mode was there any chance to come back to what was most important: the relationship.

It is unlikely that we will resolve business disputes with hugs when they end. But relationships and our sensitivity in navigating our roles in relationships routinely have a far greater impact on how or whether conflicts resolve than do the issues themselves. It is likely that we or a person we are connected to will misinterpret our roles occasionally over the duration of the relationship, and we will fight and behave in ways we wish we hadn't. If we can lower the emotional temperature, stay present, and reflect on our expectations in the relationship, then productive things can happen, and we can thoughtfully move through the conflict.

Hidden Agenda

Another, less volatile, situation with Rachel happened more recently. When I start offering unsolicited advice to my married daughters (which I misguidedly do), it's with the implicit assumption that I know better and have a right to engage in the role of tour guide. My daughters and I agree that I've long ago been assigned to the consultant stage, but I sometimes attempt to revert back to the earlier stage with neither permission nor request. It is not clever, and it is nearly always unhelpful.

When I get called out, I'm grateful…kind of…only later.

We were visiting Rachel and her husband, Ben. They have two little boys. I love to cook, and I like to watch how other people prepare food. Rachel was cutting an apple by slicing it on four sides. I cut apples differently, by quartering them and then carefully cutting the core and seeds from each quarter. I've spent way too much time thinking about the best way to cut an apple.

"Do you always cut apples like that?" I asked Rachel, as if it were nothing more than a question.

"Dad," Rachel replied without missing a beat, "I cut apples for my family every day without your help. If you have a suggestion, just make it."

She said this with a familiar and slightly irritated look.

Awareness is important. Until I was called out, I would have defended my question as nothing more than a curious inquiry. However, my question was not asked out of idle interest. It was not even a question, although the words were arranged that way. I was criticizing the way she did it, and I had an agenda to tell her how to do it "right," to move back into the tour-guide stage.

When I am engaged in an emotional conflict (and they are all emotional at some level), I may think I am drawing back to ask a question. But in fact, I'm asking a question with the agenda to change my role in the relationship without being too obvious about it. Not everyone will call me out as directly as Rachel did, but almost everyone will react negatively. I am just not that good at disguising my motives.

This is a minor but revealing example of my wanting to show what I know or tell someone else how to do something. Sometimes the issues are bigger than how to cut an apple. We all need to pay attention to the questions we ask, the nature of the relationships, and what, if anything, someone has asked of us. Being aware of our role and our responsibility in a conflict can help us do it better.

Takeaway

When we find ourselves in an external conflict, our brains are inclined to make a list of why we are right. We become self-absorbed in our own point of view and almost oblivious to the possibility that another point of view exists. Rather than moving closer to the other person, we push them away. No one is positively affected by someone else's self-absorption.

Action

The next time you are told that you "don't understand," consider whether that is true. Then ask yourself if you have made any effort to understand or have just wanted the other person to understand you and tell you that you are right. A sincere effort to understand, even if unsuccessful, can open a door for connection. It is possible to understand where someone is coming from and disagree with the underlying information that led to their conclusions. Even if you find yourself unable to understand, you can accept that they see the issue differently from you, and look for someplace to find a connection, though perhaps not about the ultimate issue.

3

The Problem of
Circumstance

The covid-19 pandemic of 2019/2020 is dominating life as I'm editing this chapter. People are full of opinions about the nature of the virus as well as the appropriate way to respond, both individually and collectively. The one irrefutable truth is that the circumstances of a pandemic affect everyone. What previously was easy has become hard, and what was already hard has become harder—the problem of circumstance.

Perspective plays a big role in how we respond to the circumstance of our lives. As my friend Rosemary told me, "The problem is not your circumstances, but what you *think* about your circumstances." Rosemary was a wise, gray-haired soul who wore red and green muumuus with flower and paisley patterns. She had lost two spouses and nearly all of her money except for a meager Social Security stipend. Yet most days, she was in good humor and largely lacking in cynicism.

One day, Rosemary commented on my dissatisfaction.

"You have the same job, the same wife, the same body, and the same beliefs as you did yesterday. And yesterday you were fine, but today you are dripping with dissatisfaction."

"No defense," I responded.

In terms of health and physical comfort, my circumstances were easier than Rosemary's, but my attitude suggested otherwise. Conflicts and circumstances are replete with comparisons. We compare ourselves with others and with what we imagine our circumstances could or should be.

An Uncommon Choice

We all have inside us a metaphorical rain barrel that is filled with our reservoir of resilience. Some of us have large barrels and some of us have small ones. At times, our life circumstances nearly drain our rain barrels, whatever the size. At other times, our circumstances leave us feeling like we are overflowing with capacity and can offer it to others.

Depending on the size of our barrels and whatever is happening at the time, we have more or less resilience to deal with conflict. Feelings are instinctive, and we cannot avoid experiencing them, but we can choose behavior that does not make us prisoners of our feelings. Being aware of our circumstances and how they affect our feelings and our reservoir of resilience will help us to avoid creating new conflicts or aggravating old ones.

Recently, I was witness to a graceful example of someone skillfully drawing on her resilience to adjust to circumstances that could have derailed her professionalism at work. Bo and Cicely were lawyers on opposite sides of a gnarly property dispute involving the sale of real estate with a business, which was aggravated by a long-tortured personal relationship between the business owners. Bo and his client wanted to have the mediation by whatever means available and be done with the issue or take it to trial. Cicely and her client felt that the only way the case could be resolved was to do it in person. On the scheduled date, a remote Zoom mediation was our only option.

Mediations, at least the thousands I have done, are nearly always done in person. The primary decision-makers and their lawyers are usually in the same place so that everyone has the benefit of using our full array of communication skills, including language, tone, body movements, gestures, and interpersonal dynamics. Something as subtle as a sigh or as obvious as crossed arms are easy to observe. The rhythm changes as we come and go at will.

The pandemic has put a stop to most in-person mediations. We are doing the majority of meetings via remote videoconferencing platforms. Some players prefer it, but many don't. The circumstance of the process itself can create conflicts.

When people disagree about the method, it is up to the judge, not the mediator, to decide how to proceed. Cicely thought that she and Bo had agreed to postpone the mediation to a later date. Bo did not think they had agreed to a postponement. I was not sure what had been decided, and I reached out to both sides the day before the mediation was to take place.

"I'm fine with postponing it or doing it by Zoom," I wrote in an email to Bo and Cicely. "I cannot do it in person. I'm assuming it is off, but if I've misunderstood, please let me know."

"The mediation is not off," Bo emailed back. "We are filing an emergency motion for the court to order the mediation to happen tomorrow morning as scheduled by Zoom."

There was no response from Cicely.

Later that evening I emailed everyone again. "Any word?" I asked. "Are we on or not?"

"We are on," Bo emailed me, attaching a copy of the judge's order requiring the mediation to take place as previously agreed.

About nine o'clock that night I got a call from Cicely. "Guess I'll see you via video at nine a.m.," she said curtly. "I was out of town all day and unaware that the motion was filed or that the judge had issued an order until just now. I'll call my client and tell her to be present."

She hung up, saying nothing further.

Having had to make those calls to clients before, I felt for Cicely needing to call her client late at night to tell her that she had to appear for something she thought would not be happening and in a way she did not prefer.

That night I went to bed thinking what a mess it would be when we got together in the morning. The clients were mad. The lawyers were mad. One lawyer thought the mediation was off, and the other convinced a judge to order it to happen. Mediating heated disputes is hard enough without circumstantial righteous arguments between lawyers who both think they are right—regardless of whether one is or isn't.

Precisely at 9:00 a.m. I opened the virtual conference room.

"Good morning, Bo," I said. "Good morning, Cicely. It's nice to see you and your clients. We agreed that you would both spend some time sharing how you see the case and how your client would like to have it resolved. Cicely, your side is first."

I felt my heart rate surge and my stomach clench, wondering what Cicely would say to Bo about the judge's order that she learned of only twelve hours before. I prepared for fireworks of righteous indignation.

"Good morning, everyone. Thank you all for being here," Cicely started. "We'd like to get this case resolved if we can. Here are some thoughts that we think will influence the outcome." Then Cicely proceeded to talk in detail about the facts and the law that she believed were important. She never mentioned the emergency request to compel the mediation, when the order happened, or when she learned of it. She shot no personal arrows at Bo.

After Cicely presented her thoughts, Bo shared his. Then I put people in separate breakout rooms, and I began with Cicely and her client.

"Cicely, I was upset *for you* not learning until late last night that today's mediation was happening," I said. "I'm sorry I could not have done more to prevent the surprise. I'm pleased that you and your client both showed up on time to mediate, but weren't you pissed? I appreciate you not bringing it up, but how did you do it?"

"I am pissed," Cicely affirmed. "Last night I was really pissed. I thought about filing my own emergency petition to have the mediation canceled."

"It was a good call not to, but how did you get there?" I wondered out loud.

"If I had said something to Bo about how he obtained an emergency order without making sure I was told, then he would have been defensive in front of his client. Once he got mad at me, I would have gotten mad back," she said with some energy. "Although we think this case has a much better chance of settling in person, that is not our option today. My client would like to settle it if we can. If I picked a fight with Bo, it would be about my ego and not my client. My job is to enhance the process, not kill it. Whether I like it doesn't matter."

"That puts you in about one percent of lawyers—not to righteously vent your spleen under those circumstances," I said.

"Thanks," she said.

We dove into the process with everyone working hard to settle the case.

This highlights one of the first problems with circumstance, and it is not reserved for lawyers. When we experience disagreement driven by righteousness and it appears at the end of a long, hard day of work, we are unavoidably affected by the circumstances of the day. We are not just tired when a hard day ends. Our resilience is low and our feeling of entitlement for relief is high. Conflict is particularly difficult as the day ends and transitions into night. Unfortunately, that is often when families come back together and adults and children alike are out of gas.

Cicely had to go through a thoughtful internal process when

she received the judge's order. She had worked out of town all day and was confronted with something she had not planned to see, didn't want to see, and required her to take immediate action. In a very short period of time, she had to make an unpleasant phone call to tell her client to appear for a mediation that her client thought was off. Then she had to prepare, clear her calendar for the next day, and appear herself first thing in the morning. In her mind, this was because Bo failed to understand what she believed was clear: the mediation was off.

Bo thought the opposite. He was clear that the mediation was not off, and he did not agree otherwise.

Now there was not only a disagreement between the clients, but between Cicely and Bo. The steps that were taken threatened to blow right through any professional trust they might have had. Regardless of any intent to violate trust, once someone feels like they have been taken advantage of, it is hard to regain the equilibrium to have helpful conversations or make good decisions.

Cicely's handling of the situation can teach us many things about conflict and the problem of circumstance. First, she acknowledged how she felt but accepted that the circumstances were what they were. What she thought about them would not change them. She did not invest in self-pity or focus on what she saw as the unfairness of the other lawyer or the judge's order. Second, in spite of feeling taken advantage of by the other lawyer, she paused to remember that her primary purpose was to further her client's interests. Indulging her sense of justice and her ego would have conflicted with her duty to her client. Finally, she not only accepted the circumstances and remembered her priorities, she also chose to behave professionally by not reacting to her feelings and scolding her counterpart. In short, she had the resilience to feel one way and act another.

Symptom or Disease?

For most of us the problem of circumstance is closer to home. Sometimes we become so focused on the difficulty we perceive in our circumstances with our families that we miss a larger issue. Circumstances always matter, but how they matter can vary.

Darby and Raul recently became empty nesters. Their household consisted of the two of them and their rescued beagle, Gilligan. Just after their youngest son left for college, Darby's father died, and her mother, Kay, was diagnosed with early Alzheimer's disease and came to *temporarily* live with them. Darby is a hospital administrator and leaves early for work five days a week. Raul is a graphic artist and works from home. Before Kay moved in, Raul and Darby had created an office in their living room where Raul spent most days designing while Gilligan slept on the couch.

Darby returned home from work one evening after Kay had been living with them for nearly six months. Kay was asleep, snoring on the couch with Gilligan sleeping next to her.

"How was your day?" Darby asked.

"How do you think?" Raul answered.

"You don't have to be so pissy," Darby said. She pointed to her mom and Gilligan sound asleep. "How cute are those two?"

"Not as cute as you think if you were here trying to work with them all day," Raul said. "When this began, you promised no more than a month; it's been six."

"We just haven't found the right living situation for her," Darby responded a bit defensively.

"That's because no care facility is good enough for you," Raul said. "We've looked at six within fifteen miles."

"Someone has to be here with her, and my job won't allow for me to do that. Besides, I make twice as much money as you, so this just makes sense," Darby said, wishing she could pull the last sentence back.

"So that's what this is about!" Raul yelled, waking both Kay and Gilligan.

"I'm really sorry," Darby said. "I didn't mean that."

"I love your mother," Raul said, through clenched teeth, "but I didn't sign up to be a full-time caretaker and to be insulted by you." He stormed out of the room.

Darby stood there as Gilligan sidled up to her leg and Kay looked blankly at Darby from the couch.

"How did we get here?" Darby said to herself.

What we think about our circumstances is unavoidably affected by the context of our conflicts. The thing about circumstances is that the presenting circumstance is sometimes the symptom and not the disease. What appeared to be about a difficult life circumstance regarding Darby's aging mother revealed a larger conflict between Darby and Raul and their perceptions of the roles they played in their marriage.

Darby and Raul found a place for Kay to move that worked for all of them. And because they paid attention to the fact that an issue larger than the circumstances of Kay living with them was at play in their conflict, they also found a marriage therapist.

Miscommunication

By definition, people who hire lawyers to sue one another are dissatisfied with some circumstance in their lives. They are so dissatisfied that they will spend lots of time and money to hire a lawyer to fight a battle for them with no guarantee of an outcome. They are often sure that the world (or a judge or jury) could not see something differently from them, so they give up all agency and turn the entire decision-making process over to strangers.

How people feel at the end of that process varies just as much as the human beings involved. If they win, then justice was done. If they lose, then justice was denied. Gene and Casey are two men in the same lawsuit who reached different conclusions about their circumstances.

Gene and Casey had been next-door neighbors for forty years. Both were widowers, and their wives had been close friends. Gene and Casey did not dislike each other, but they didn't have much of a relationship after their wives passed. Gene was selling his house and had a survey done to prepare for the sale. According to the survey, Casey's fence in the backyard was six inches on Gene's property.

Gene, thinking there would be no issue, sent Casey an email showing him the survey. At the end of the email he said, "Please let me know if you can move your fence by the end of the month when I put my house up for sale." Gene thought he was being generous.

Casey was immediately offended that Gene did not come to talk with him. Casey sent an email in return that said, "My fence has been there for forty years. I have no plans to move it now or in the future. I'm happy to discuss it with whoever buys the house from you."

Gene responded, "I never would have thought you'd be this kind of problem. Move the fence or I'll have my son come and take it down. It's on my property."

Casey sent back, "If your son touches my fence, I'll call the sheriff. I'm going to have my own survey done."

"Here is my survey," Casey's next email began. "I'll move my fence when you tear out your concrete driveway that is on my property and pay to landscape my yard."

Casey's survey showed that his fence was only two inches on Gene's property in the backyard and also that Gene's driveway, in the front yard, was two feet on Casey's property.

The lines were drawn. The emails stopped as the lawyers were engaged.

Gene and Casey both hired good lawyers. The lawyers told each of them that they could win all, or part, or none of their claims. The lawyers independently advised their clients to work it out. Gene and Casey did not work it out, and they came to see me with their lawyers for a pre-suit mediation, before full-blown litigation prevented any face-saving alternative.

The lawyers warned me of the dynamic ahead of time and suggested that Gene and Casey not be together.

"We are here because the judge ordered us to be here," Casey said when I entered the room. "There is no compromise. Gene is the son of a bitch that started this without the courtesy of a call or a knock on my front door. We are taking this to the mat."

Casey went further into detail, getting angrier and angrier while his lawyer looked at his hands. Casey did not care that the cost of litigation was more than any possible remedy to the problem. He was invested in his resentment.

When I walked into Gene's room, it was quiet.

"Who wants to begin?" I asked, looking at Gene and his lawyer.

Gene lifted his head and spoke.

"When this began, all I could think about was how Casey had taken advantage of me for forty years by putting that fence on my property. He never surveyed it and just put it where he wanted. If I'd died on the property, I'd never have known. Once I had it surveyed and learned that it was on my property, I sent him the email without thinking. I knew I was right and thought he'd move the fence."

I looked at him but said nothing.

"I have no interest in talking to Casey," Gene said, "but give him whatever he wants. He can leave the fence, I'll move my driveway. I'd buy him a Big Mac and a bus ticket just to be done.

"This process is so miserable," Gene continued, "If I'd had any idea of the amount of anxiety this would cause, I would never have begun. I'm tired of lawyers and arguing. The price on me is way too high."

His lawyer then talked with me about how we might have the conversation and get the dispute buttoned up.

Perception is everything. When the circumstances first arose,

Gene attributed selfish motives and disrespect to Casey. When Gene sent an email, Casey felt insulted and fired back. In this case, the only thing that changed about the circumstances was what Casey and Gene both thought about them. Casey was determined to prove his point, and Gene could not come up with any point that made it worth continuing the fight.

Only because one of the parties decided it wasn't worth it did this dispute end.

Perspectives about circumstances are frequently miscommunicated or misheard in writing. Body language, tone, and timing are easy to imply or miss. Our tendency to trust the way we view a situation leads us to think someone else reads it the same way. Alternatively, we may be afraid that someone does, in fact, see it differently, and we send a letter to avoid a face-to-face conversation. It can be that the message creates or aggravates a conflict that could have been easily resolved in person. Before asking someone to do something in writing, think about whether you might be better off setting up a time to see them in person rather than risk the circumstance of getting your wires crossed. Then be prepared to listen.

My Space or Yours?

Entitlement has everything to do with expectations and nothing to do with needs. We all like to be respected, and we attach some perks or circumstances to that respect.

Case in point. Our office has two parking lots, a very large one out front and a small six-car lot just by the door to the lobby. These six convenient spots were originally assigned by seniority, and I've had one for a long time. The spots were allocated so long ago that some younger partners did not even know they had been informally assigned.

For six months, I'd been walking to work instead of driving, so *my* spot had been routinely empty. One of the younger partners began parking in *my* space. She has a young family and is often shooting in and out of the office and slogging all sorts of paraphernalia, so it makes sense for the spot to be used.

However, I wanted to be noticed and thanked, so one night when she was leaving at the same time I was, I said, "So you've taken my spot."

"I didn't know there were assigned spots," she replied quizzically.

"No problem. If I want it back, I'll let you know," I said, as if I were being generous.

I walked home embarrassed for having brought it up.

The next day, she came to my office and said, "I woke up last night thinking about our conversation. If I'm out of line, I want to apologize. I don't have to claim that space."

"I left yesterday embarrassed for saying anything," I said. "It was small of me. You should have the space. It needs to be used, and I don't need it. Please use it."

We have had several pleasant exchanges since then, but it took weeks of the space being vacant before she felt comfortable using it again, in spite of my urging. Had I simply been quiet, I could have squelched my embarrassing need for credit and not cost her a wink of sleep.

The parking space issue will not change anyone's lives. Whether my grown-up, thinly disguised temper tantrum about a parking space was driven by my ego, entitlement, or just a confluence of circumstances, I don't know. However, as we unconsciously weave entitlement into our circumstances, it can reveal parts of us that are best hidden or dispensed with altogether.

One thing we can do is think about whether we are asking questions because we have an honest and benign curiosity or whether the question itself is attention-seeking behavior because we are unwilling to say what is really on our minds…perhaps because it shouldn't be said.

Fighting or Surrendering to Circumstance

Conflict awaits us in predictable and unpredictable ways. It is unavoidable. With some conflicts, the circumstances are transient and occupy little space in our thoughts. In other cases, the circumstances surrounding conflicts are big enough that they take up lots of space in our heads and can seem overwhelming and beyond our capacity to live through them. As we think about conflicts, large or small, it is tempting to allow our fear to push us to a fight-or-flight mode.

A couple of years ago, a dear friend received a devastating medical diagnosis. Before he was to have surgery, Patty and I flew out to visit with him and his wife.

On the Sunday morning we were to return home, our friend invited us to join him and his wife on a conference call with Amit Sood, a medical colleague who had served on the staff at the Mayo Clinic for many years. Dr. Sood has refocused his professional life on helping people find the resilience to be stronger, kinder, and happier. You can read more about his work at his website *Resilient Option* at www.resilientoption.com.

Dr. Sood listened to the fears and anxiety that our friends were experiencing. He also listened to the concerns Patty and I had about our newly married daughter who had recently been diagnosed with cancer. One of Patty's frustrations with well-meaning friends and even healthcare providers was the phrase "fight the cancer" or "beat the cancer." There was something about those phrases that reduced those who died from their cancer to people who had somehow constitutionally or morally failed to survive. It just didn't feel right.

Dr. Sood listened intently. Then in a kind and caring voice he offered the same counsel to both of our families.

"I agree that asking people who are suffering from a serious and scary diagnosis to 'fight' is not the best advice," he began. "People can be well-meaning and still unhelpful. I'd suggest that you turn over the fight to people who have the tools and the training to fight. In my mind that includes the doctors and everyone on the healthcare team whose profession it is to deal with the circumstance of the disease. They are in the disease-fighting business. By surrendering the fight, you can do the things that are designed to feed you on a difficult journey."

He suggested four things:

1. Invest in the people you care about and who nourish you.

2. Read things that are important to you and that encourage peace and joy.

3. Pray or think about another person in a focused way for twenty minutes every day.

4. Engage in a cause or an act of service that is bigger than you.

Dr. Sood did not suggest that there was anything unusual about our choices in responding to our circumstances, but he presented the option to offload the fight response to someone better equipped to handle it. Once the decision is made to transfer the fight to someone else, then we can focus on fostering our resilience to move through our difficult circumstances.

Any one of the four actions Dr. Sood proposes better equips us to replenish our resilience. The tools can be used in small or large ways on a daily basis. Using them is similar to an athlete or musician training for an event or performance. We would not be good teammates if we did not prepare for the game. We would not be good performers if we did not practice. Self-care before the conflict presents itself seems a worthy expenditure of time.

Circumstances that include suffering await us all, but they do not have to dictate our response. To behave differently from how our circumstances lead us to feel takes sustained effort, and we will not always have the will or the strength to do it. An empty resilience barrel may leave us needing to borrow from others. Viktor Frankl in his book *Man's Search for Meaning*, about his experience in concentration camps in World War II, suggests that we have a choice. "Everything can be taken from a man but one thing: the last of the human freedoms—to choose one's attitude in any given set of circumstances, to choose one's own way."[1]

There can be a problem with circumstance, but it does not need to define us. I'm drawn to the old adage "*It* may not be OK, but *we* can be."

Takeaway

Circumstances influence us, but they do not have to control us. In times when our circumstances overwhelm us, it is important not to expect our best instincts to emerge. It is OK to put important decisions off until we have the resources to address them. It is equally important to recognize how circumstance might be affecting those with whom we are in conflict, so we can give them the benefit of the doubt and not expect the best from them. Sometimes we may need to loan some of our resilience to them, without expecting a payback. It may be that the only power we can reclaim in times of suffering is our power to choose our attitude.

Action

When you feel spent by your circumstances and you have nothing left to give, be wary of entering into contentious conversations to make important decisions. If someone innocently tries to draw you in, you might find yourself inclined to snap at them or

---

1   Viktor Frankl, *Man's Search for Meaning*, 4th ed. (Boston: Beacon Press, 1992), 75.

make a snide comment to push them away. When you recognize this feeling, try saying, "I'm sorry I don't have the energy to have this conversation right now, but I'm happy to revisit it tomorrow or next week." Then make it a point to bring up the conversation in the time you suggested.

4

The Justice Gene

The justice gene is embedded deep within us all. No scientific research has yet uncovered it, but it resides in some recess of our mind, spirit, or soul. It shapes our sense of right and wrong and compels us to righteously defend our beliefs. You may call it a moral compass, and, indeed, it directs us to justify our actions, rationalize our behavior, and engage in conflict with those who fall on the other side of our strongly held opinions. It presents as instinct: we just *know* it. The thinking part of the justice gene comes after we first feel it.

We are as unaware of the justice gene as we are of our bodies when they are not in use. When we sit on the front porch, listening to a summer rain and daydreaming, we do not notice our leg or head or hand, unless something changes. We suddenly feel a shooting pain on our right hand and look down as a wasp flies away. Now we become acutely aware of our hand, the pain, and the cause of the pain.

The justice gene works similarly. It lies unnoticed until something stings it.

You know that your justice gene has been stung when the words "that's not fair" enter your mind or escape your lips. Fairness lurks in nearly every aspect of conflict, and, in fact, our sense of what is fair or unfair is very frequently the genesis of conflict. Though we cannot always explain why we feel something is fair or unfair, our belief in our perspective is nearly unshakeable.

The justice gene presents us with internal conflicts when no one else is around, as our behavior clashes with our priorities. It drives external conflicts as we engage others who are wrestling with their own demons, demanding fairness that doesn't align with ours. If you disagree, consider how many times, in your mind or out loud, you have said, "That's not fair," or "Things should be different," or "You ought to do this."

Often, while in the midst of conflict, it feels like justice has left the building and we are standing alone. It is scary in a primal way. Our reaction to unfairness and injustice is instinctive—we feel the unfairness physically, and our brain chemistry kicks into action. Our faces flush, our hearts pound, our palms sweat, and we prepare to fight. It's an all-hands-on-deck adrenaline rush. When the justice gene is assaulted (no matter the reason), it is not a thoughtful process.

One reason that our physiological reaction to injustice is so compelling is that anger is energizing, leading us to believe (often falsely) that we have more power than we do. Anger can justify almost any response to a situation. Have you ever noticed that when someone is angry with you, your own response is to reciprocate in kind with anger? That is a power-to-power protective mechanism that's hard to sidestep. Sometimes it's an appropriate response when personal or emotional safety is threatened or when standing up to power is a scary but essential option. Other times, dueling justice genes will push you to fight it out without regard to consequence, and the conflict rarely ends well.

In nearly every conflict, our justice gene has been punched, and the only positive way to move forward is to let the swelling go down until we are not so blinded by our initial assessment. We might return to it and find the conflict needs to go to trial, the divorce needs to happen, or the business needs to close. However, engaging in conflict in the midst of an adrenaline-fueled rage rarely leads to good decisions or outcomes.

Neutral parties can certainly be helpful when you're having a hard time distancing yourself from the heavy emotions of conflict. When we find our emotions captured by anger, it is valuable to ask for the perspective of someone in our lives who will be honest with us. First, to sort out whether an injustice actually occurred. Second, to help us put the experience and our response in perspective.

The Big Picture

Daily we reach unilateral conclusions based on flawed perspectives and inconclusive evidence. Yet we hold on to our conclusions with the emotional and intellectual power of a shark with a seal in its jaws. Deep in our bones our instincts tell us that objective fairness exists, and we believe we're able to recognize it, so we need to hold on tight to it. The problem is that what we see as objective is always viewed through our subjective lens, and that lens is not all-seeing. By its nature it crops out some of the scene, obstructing our view of the big picture, making us vulnerable to reaching incorrect conclusions about a situation based on incomplete information, leading us into conflict.

Sometimes the limits of our perspective can trigger our justice gene while watching something as seemingly uncontroversial as a ten-year-old's basketball game.

"Are you excited?" I asked Grace.

"Not really," she answered, leaning against her purple travel bag in the passenger seat of our old Camry.

It was 6:30 Sunday morning, and we were driving two hours to New Castle for an Amateur Athletic Union basketball tournament. AAU was the travel league divided by gender and age groups for

aspiring basketball players who were interested in competing beyond their local communities.

That was not us. Grace had good friends who played basketball
well, and she was invited by a wonderfully inclusive coach, Jack,
to be on the team. He coached the girls with equal care and en-
thusiasm, whether they were future college prospects or were not
destined to play beyond elementary school. A couple of the girls
were really good, the rest average to below average. But they liked
one another and had a lot of fun on a team the girls had named the
Purple Grapes.

"If she's not excited," I wondered to myself, "then why did I get
up at 5:30 a.m. to make sandwiches, load the car, and get her up for
a two-hour drive?"

Grace slept for the whole two hours while I drove on in the
cold, dark February morning.

At the tournament, Bob, the father of Tricia, another girl on the
team, sat next to me. We expected to play four games in the tournament. The gym was a former high-school bowl with old win-
dows at the top and sloped wooden bleachers that angled down
to the court. The capacity was 2,500, but there were only fifteen
parents in the stands watching their daughters play.

Bob leaned over. "Do you think we might score ten points this
game?"

"That's a fair question," I responded. "We didn't score ten points
in the last two games combined."

We were terrible, and as the second half began, our team was
behind 20–2. We scored no points at all in the first quarter. I felt
humiliated, but the girls seemed fine.

The Purple Grapes got the ball to begin the second half, and the
opposing team was pressing our girls in the backcourt. We could
not even get the ball in bounds. The ball was intercepted, and an
impressive player for the other team scored two more points: 22–2.

On the next possession the same thing happened: 24–2. My
blood started to boil with the unfairness of it. The other team was

just rubbing it in. On the third possession, we got the ball inbounds, but another player stole it and scored: 26–2. I could no longer sit quietly on my hands and watch this kind of unsporting behavior from our opponents. I stood up.

"What the heck are you doing?" I yelled at the other team's coach, a young woman who volunteered her time to coach these girls. "Can't you see you're already up 26–2?"

All eyes were on me, and the gym was completely silent.

Coach Jack looked up at me and said quietly but firmly, "Sam, I asked the other coach to press us so we could practice on it."

The gym stayed silent, and I wanted to crawl under the bleachers.

The situation had seemed clear to me: the other coach was using this occasion to dominate and humiliate a team that was not up to her team's level of competition. This was not what ten-year-old recreational basketball was about.

My only perspective was mine, and the injustice was evident. It had never occurred to me that Jack had asked the other coach to press our team so we could practice and get better. We were never going to win the game, but the girls on the Purple Grapes could learn some new skills, Jack believed.

After the game, I also learned that the other coach had protested Jack's request to press. She did not want to give any impression that she was trying to run up the score. She did it only at Jack's insistence.

I was the only one in the gym who felt compelled to vent his spleen about what was happening to our team, and I was totally wrong. My anger, ignited by my offended justice gene, was incapable of imagining any scenario where what I was watching was OK. I self-righteously yelled at an innocent volunteer coach who was only doing what had been requested of her, and the one humiliated was me (and, I learned later, Grace).

When the game was over, I had recovered enough from my embarrassment to apologize to the other coach and to Jack. After the tournament, Grace and I drove home. Mostly in silence.

"Dad, what were you thinking!" Grace finally said, not really asking.

"Sometimes I'm just an idiot," I said.

Any explanation would have been no more than a useless excuse. "If you can't be a good example," my wife says, "then you'll just have to be a horrible warning."

It can be helpful to be aware that what we *want* nearly always aligns with what we think is *fair*. By marrying desire to justice, I can transform what I want into an entitlement. If my entitlement becomes grounded in a moral imperative and is still denied, then it is easy to be resentful in a way that primarily hurts me but can also harm others. My first misstep on the day of the AAU tournament was asking a sleepy ten-year-old whether she was excited to be in the car at 6:30 in the morning in an attempt to make myself feel better. I felt entitled to some gratitude from Grace, and I began unconsciously harboring resentment that I was spending a Sunday doing something that Grace was not that excited about.

I failed to notice that once we were there, Grace was clearly having fun with her friends. Resentment is like the sugar rush of conflict. It lingers but almost always with negative side-effects that drain our energy away from things like the fact that there is always a perspective different from our own. As I allowed the resentment to settle in, unrecognized, my justice gene was primed for aggravation. So when I believed that my daughter and her team were not only being disrespected but also humiliated, it was a short jump for me to unthinkingly, and mistakenly, demand fairness, embarrassing more than just myself. Limited information paired with resentment is a bad recipe for engaging with conflict positively.

Although this was a small AAU tournament twenty years ago and probably quickly forgotten by everyone else, I have not forgotten and don't want to. When I feel the rage of righteous anger, I always want to pause and consider the next thing I am about to say or do. My perspective could be wrong, I could be resentful about something else entirely, or I could be hungry and tired.

Even if it's none of those things, my response could be unhelpful, or even dangerous. Merely making the effort to understand how someone else sees fairness can transition us from reaction to response and into quiet consideration. Among the most important things we can do if we value relationships at work and at home is to graciously get over our resentments so that the more sensitive elements of our nature, like our justice gene, aren't so vulnerable to attack.

Principles

No matter how many times our parents tell us "the world isn't fair," we cling to the hope that it is. We want to believe that perfect justice and fairness exist somewhere. Not only that, but if perfect justice and fairness exist, then there can be no disagreement, because one person would clearly be right, and the other person would clearly be wrong. In fact, our ideas about justice, fairness, and principles are so deeply interwoven into who we are that anything that threatens those ideas pushes us away from engagement. We then have two sides standing toe-to-toe, arguing with a moral commitment that is unwavering.

People hold on to principles with nearly the same ferocity that they would hold on to a child being pulled away by a stranger. Justice is religion, even for those who don't have a religion. Who doesn't want what is fair, and how can you argue with my belief in fairness? Listening is for other people. "All I want is what is fair," two people proclaim as they define "fair" in dramatically different ways.

People come to my office to mediate their disagreements about what is fair. Individuals and companies hire lawyers to redress the ways they believe they have been wronged. The legal issues range from medical malpractice cases to corporate contract disputes to siblings dividing their parents' estates. The fights I mediate nearly always involve lawsuits, but the way people feel about their own righteousness is the same whether in the living room or in the courtroom.

When people arrive for a mediation, I give the separate parties and their lawyers their own rooms. Before we begin, I enter each room to meet the people and discuss the process.

One day I walked into the room and met Hazel, who immediately said, "I'm not greedy. All I want is what's fair." Then she said, "I'm not the suing kind," and meant it.

"It's nice to meet you, Hazel," I greeted her. "I take it that this is your first lawsuit. Am I right?" We discussed what happens at a mediation, and I told her I was going down the hall to meet the other folks.

"All I want is what's fair," Simon said as I entered the room down the hall. "Hazel cheated me out of my bonus, and I'll spend whatever it takes to get what's mine. It's not about the money; it's about the principle!"

"Nice to meet you, Simon," I said. "This lawsuit business is not much fun, but we settle cases about ninety-eight percent of the time. I see no reason why we can't do that today."

We also talked about the process.

After addressing the preliminaries, we all gathered in a large room for the lawyers to share their conflicting perspectives. I sat at the end of the table. Hazel and Simon sat across from each other, with their lawyers next to them.

Simon's lawyer finished with, "Hazel actually stole Simon's bonus, and she should not only pay the bonus, but pay more for punishment and then pay my attorney fees."

Hazel's lawyer countered, "Simon is the worst human resources person in the history of Hazel's company. Not only does Hazel owe Simon nothing, he owes her money."

Another typical day of mediation begins.

Here is the unsettling part: I was someone who did not have a dog in the fight, and Simon and Hazel and their lawyers were equally convincing. They had facts to support their competing

views of Simon's time at the company, and they each had witnesses. They were deeply committed to their versions of fairness, based on their truths. They were convinced that they were
right, and no one was going to persuade them that they were
wrong...including me.

Our arguments, which we so heavily lean on, are seldom per-
suasive to anyone who does not already agree with us. Yet we argue
until we are blue in the face. For thirty-five years I have worked as
an advocate for one party or another in litigation, or as a mediator
working with all sides of a conflict to find a way to settle a lawsuit.
If both sides are determined to convince the other side they are
wrong, we may as well march into the parking lot and throw rocks
at each other. After all, if both sides are certain they're right, hurling
stones is likely to be as influential as any professional tactic I could
employ.

So why do cases settle?

Simon's and Hazel's case settled for the same reasons that all
cases settle—it makes sense to the people involved. But this case,
like many, did not settle before we had a conversation about principles in both rooms. Principles are the values we use to hold on to
our beliefs about what is fair.

"Hazel, you told me in no uncertain terms that principles are
important to you. Whatever else might happen, you are not going
to compromise your principles. Did I hear that correctly?" I asked.

"You sure did," Hazel said, almost before I could finish.

"Your lawyer agreed that there are two options: settle this case
today or take it to trial, right?" I asked.

"Yes, and I'd rather have a jury tell me I'm wrong than compromise with Simon."

"Let's talk about that a minute. Is that OK with you?"

"OK," Hazel crossed her arms, looking wary.

"Do you remember when we talked about risk? Even though
you know you are right, your lawyer said that there is at least a
twenty percent chance that a jury could get it wrong for reasons we

never could predict. We lawyers are oddsmakers, but we cannot promise results."

"Yes," Hazel acknowledged, although she clearly could not imagine a jury getting it wrong.

"In fact," I went on, "one side or the other always thinks the jury got it wrong—that justice was not done."

"Maybe," Hazel said slowly.

"Well, here is my question, Hazel. This is a conversation I have with people nearly every day, so you are in a club of capable, smart people who find themselves in lawsuits that they never dreamed could happen," I said.

"Let's say that the twenty percent bad result happens. Let's say that there is a group of jurors who really identify with Simon, ignore the facts, and come back with a verdict against you and for Simon. I know that you don't think it will happen, but let's say it does."

Hazel just looked at me, shaking her head.

"If that happens, if the jury gets it wrong, are your principles going to change?"

"Hell no!" Hazel said.

"Damn straight," I confirmed. "Because your principles are too important to turn over to a group of strangers, aren't they?"

"That's right," Hazel said, but this time more quietly.

"One other thing," I said. "If you win, as you believe you will, do you think Simon's principles are going to change?"

"No way," Hazel said. "He doesn't have any principles."

"I'm not asking you or Simon to change your principles. They are too important, and I have no right to do that. Even though we call it the 'justice system,' someone nearly always leaves resenting the fact that justice was not done. At least that has been my experience," I said.

I had a nearly identical conversation with Simon.

Why have I gone into such a long story about the principles of mediation? Because our deep, instinctive, emotional commitment to our clear-eyed view of justice is not something we are going to allow anyone to argue us out of. It is too entrenched, too personal, and too scary to let go of. But in the middle of a conflict, most of us behave as if our arguments and negotiating skills are going to change someone else's mind. We are nearly always wrong. Sometimes the alternative to demanding justice is to realize that what we think we are fighting for is beyond our reach. We need to pause and reflect on what we can and cannot control. We can almost never control how someone else responds. So unless we can consider other approaches and develop alternative tools, we will be like two boxers strapped together with nothing to do but punch each other in the mouth.

Tradeoffs

When conflict happens, we are confronted with loss. It is the loss of the way we think things *should* be. Whether we are toddlers, teenagers, or adult litigants, we have expectations and a sense of entitlement about the actions and behaviors of others. When people or events don't meet our expectations or when we don't get what we want, we experience grief.

Elisabeth Kübler-Ross many years ago identified the five stages of grief: denial, anger, bargaining, depression, and acceptance. The first two stages, denial and anger, nearly always apply to the justice gene. First, we cannot believe that someone sees justice differently from the way we do. We might think it's just a misunderstanding and we can easily clear things up if we simply *explained* ourselves better. When that doesn't work and we see that the other person is as committed to their perspective as we are to ours, it's easy to get angry. We bargain, we get depressed, and then (perhaps) we accept.

But the notion that there are tradeoffs when it comes to justice seems just plain wrong. We are captured by the natural "reasonableness" of the lens through which we see the world, and we are invariably surprised when someone suggests that their "fair" makes more sense than ours. It is not just that we don't understand that someone could see what is fair differently from the way we do, we don't even try to see it their way.

We see clashes over fairness in everything, from road rage to lawsuits to schoolyard fights. Some of the most difficult cases my partner and I mediate involve family members fighting over a parent's estate. The challenge bears no relationship to the money involved because it is about dramatically different views of what is fair in the context of the intimacy between family members.

A client of mine, Frank, contacted me after his wife, Gloria, had died. It was a second marriage for both of them, but they were married to each other for more than thirty years. Frank had no children, and Gloria had two. Frank and Gloria lived in Gloria's home, where she had raised the children from her first marriage. Though the children were grown and out of the house by the time Frank and Gloria married, he got along well with them and had built a good relationship as their stepfather. They were the only children he had known.

Frank and Gloria mostly kept their finances separate, but they had decided to put the house in joint ownership. When they married, the house was fully paid for. Frank transferred an amount of money equal to half the home's value into an account that Gloria had, so they were equally invested. He and Gloria used the new account for everything from vacations to helping grandchildren attend college. They never discussed it with Gloria's children. Gloria detailed in her will that she was leaving her half of the home to Frank, and all of her other assets (much more significant than the value of the home) to her children.

Not long after Gloria died, Frank decided to move, and he put the house up for sale. Gloria's son and daughter, Nick and Sarah, came to see him to make sure he would be giving them "their half" after it was sold. He was surprised and said to them, "No. Your mom and I discussed this and decided that the first to die would leave the entire value of the house to the other."

Nick and Sarah begged to differ. They told Frank it was unfair, and there was no way their mother would have wanted that. They said she had never told them about the arrangement and seemed doubtful that Frank was being honest about it. Frank told them he was sorry but remained firm: "That is what we agreed." Fortunately for Frank, it was also what her will said.

Frank, Nick, and Sarah were all hurt.

Things became even more heated. Nick and Sarah screamed at Frank that they never should have trusted him and stormed out of the house, slamming the door behind them. Frank yelled back and threw a coffee cup on the floor, shattering it. In a moment of hurt feelings and misunderstanding, the good relationships they had built, all the years of trust and understanding, had evaporated. Nick and Sarah decided that Frank had enough money on his own, and whatever was their mother's share of the house should rightfully be theirs. Frank and Gloria had worked out their finances and had no idea that Nick and Sarah would be hurt or angry. Frank, Gloria, Nick, and Sarah all acted on what they thought was fair and had no idea that any of them might see things differently. Once it was clear that they viewed the issue incompletely and through different lenses, their justice genes kicked in to damage the relationship.

Whoever we feel was "right" in this circumstance, no person in the mix was willing or able to pause and listen. Instead, they allowed fear, anger, and uncertainty to control their reactions. Their bodies and minds responded as if the lion were threatening them, and the chemicals coursing through their bodies fueled their reactions. The fight-or-flight instinct of their amygdala (primitive reactionary brain) drove their behavior, and the executive functioning of their frontal lobes took a back seat. They all paid a high price. Being open to the possibility that they might be missing something was the furthest thing from their minds. Sadly, I have seen families permanently end fifty years of joyous celebrations as they reacted to incomplete information and imputed motives.

After it became apparent that a solution was not within reach,

Frank came to see me and opened with a loaded question: "What do you think?"

"What do you mean?" I asked, trying to delay my response.

"You know what I mean," said Frank. "Who's right?"

"Do you really want to know what I think, or do you just want me to be on your side?" I asked.

I knew that Frank was grieving and also suffering from the sense of loss stemming from the conflict with Gloria's children. If I agreed with him, I would be helping him confirm his judgment of them. If I disagreed with him, I would be aggravating the conflict in his mind. If we get mired in the circumstances and focus on who is right or wrong, we miss the point and conflict remains a burning ember to be flamed.

"Let's talk about what you want, Frank," I said.

"I want to do what Gloria and I agreed, and for Nick and Sarah to accept that and get over it so we can go back to what it was before," Frank replied.

"What do you think the chances are that Nick and Sarah will get over it?"

"Maybe not much, but they should."

"Can you control how they respond?"

"Probably not."

"So let's talk about what you want most and what you are willing or unwilling to do to get it," I suggested.

After we talked more, Frank decided to see if Nick and Sarah would meet with him. Frank was devastated by Gloria's death, and his feelings were hurt that Nick and Sarah thought he was greedy. He did not need the money to live the rest of his life, and yet he thought it was fair to do what he and Gloria had agreed. Frank also knew that what might be *fair* could forever end the relationship with Nick and Sarah, which he had treasured. If they met, Frank had to decide whether his purpose was to convince Nick and Sarah of what was *fair* or whether it was to explore the possibility that the relationship could be repaired.

Nick and Sarah agreed to meet with Frank.

Frank began with an apology that contained no explanation or excuse. He said straightforwardly, "I love both of you and am very sorry that as we both grieve the loss of your mother anything has come between us. I'm happy to explain how your mother and I arranged things during our marriage and let the two of you decide what you think is best to do with the money from the house. I'm also happy to explain nothing, and I'll accept whatever you decide is the best thing to do with the money." Frank had decided what was most important to him and also decided that he would work to surrender his resentment rather than demand that Nick and Sarah get over theirs. The three of them still have a relationship.

Parking Space Humility

When it comes to fairness, proceed with caution. Who among us is not offended when we are accused of being unfair or unjust? The fear, uncertainty, and judgment that comes when we label someone "unfair" can wipe away years of history. In that moment, we trust our immediate judgment of some perceived flawed behavior and ignore the years of trust, respect, and love that suggest the other party has a long track record of kindness and decency.

Something to look for is when you find yourself demonizing the other person as one-dimensional, irredeemable, and evil. If you want to balance whatever you believe about another human being, you might consider that all of us are better than the worst thing we have ever done and not as good as the best thing we have ever done. If I can forgive myself for lapses, might I also be able to forgive someone else? This is an easy concept to abandon when someone stomps on your justice gene.

Any successful conflict engagement requires one side or the other to at least suspend their notion of fairness and avoid acting on impulse long enough to consider making a choice. We don't have to completely abandon our sense of fairness, but we have to be open to accepting alternative views if we wish to engage effectively with conflict. We do not have to forget our principles just because justice is denied. Rather, when considered more broadly, notions of fairness can transcend the tightly guarded justice gene. Putting our justice gene temporarily on hold is a conscious choice. Giving up our *right to be right* is a colossal ask; after all, it doesn't seem fair. But fairness is always in context.

Humility and compassion are not at the top of my mind when someone close to me has done something I think is unfair. Being humble about my conclusions and generous toward them are at the bottom of the list. But humility allows me to be open to the possibility that I might be wrong and permits me to consider the other person's point of view more generously. And compassion encourages me to remember that we all do the best we can, and sometimes our best is not very good. In short, humility allows me to listen, and compassion allows me to connect. Choosing to prioritize humility and compassion when deeply engaged in conflict may be the single best thing I can do. This choice doesn't guarantee my hoped-for outcome, but it does set me up for a greater chance at sustaining relationships and lowering my blood pressure.

Even when there are significant injuries to our justice gene, such as often happens in work or family situations, there are other helpful things to consider. For me, one such situation involved a coworker who had financial and family issues. He often came to work late, and when he did show up, his contributions were marginal and sometimes negative.

I complained to a different coworker, who said, "If you think it's hard for you, how hard must it be for him?" Very rarely is my first response to think about the other person who has offended me and what might underlie their "misguided" thinking. But just making the effort to understand, even if understanding remains elusive, can change the dynamic. The question my colleague asked has been enormously helpful in any number of circumstances that I experience as unfair.

One final story to illustrate the shifting notions of fairness and how we choose to respond.

Our local YMCA has woefully insufficient parking at peak times. One day, I saw someone going to their car and stopped in the driving lane with my turn signal on to let those behind me know that I was waiting for the spot. Just as the person backed out and opened the space, someone pulled to my left and took it.

I screamed curse words at the person who ignored parking lot etiquette and swooped in to take the space that was "mine." I was waiting for the driver to get out of the car so I could tell them, with outrage, the full extent of their unfairness.

Then I saw the disability license plate and an older woman get out of the car and open the trunk to get a wheelchair out to help her husband get out of the passenger seat. I was glad it was winter so no one could have heard my vulgar outburst. I drove on with a face red with embarrassment rather than rage.

Dealing with the nuance of what is fair is really hard. Prioritizing responses to assaults on the justice gene is another important skill for engaging with conflict well. Not all injustices are created equal: some cost lives and others cost nothing but our pride. If lives or significant opportunities are at risk, then the alarm bells need to be honored. If the tweak to fairness is only that someone took "your" parking spot, it is time to accept it and let the adrenaline dissipate.

I've said it before, but it bears repeating—being right is really expensive and way overrated. Being right often causes pain. Being right damages relationships. Always remember that when you insist on your own rightness, you run the risk of being proven wrong and weakening connections.

Watch Your Privilege

As we've been discussing, fairness and justice are often, though not always, in the eye of the beholder. The person who benefits from the privilege justifies it, and the person who doesn't feels wronged.

Although it is a topic for a larger book, it is important to remember that there are whole groups of people who systemically receive unfair treatment. The law allows for "protected classes" of people who cannot be discriminated against for certain traits, such as race, gender, sexual orientation, age, or religion, but not every person who has been discriminated against can afford a lawyer to take up their case. Systemic unfairness creates a multitude of social injustices that can lead people who experience it to lose hope and establish different survival strategies. It often makes sense to those who feel like the game is fixed against them to hold tightly to whatever allows them to feel less unsafe and not risk losing it in a system that has consistently diminished them in some way. Systemic injustices affect opportunity, health, and life itself. People who feel trapped in a web of unfairness commonly experience chronic sadness, disappointment, anger, and despair that can become part of their DNA.

On the other hand, those who repeatedly benefit from the system may come to feel entitled to those benefits to such an extent that any slight injustice incites them to demand what they believe is rightfully theirs. They often use the considerable power at their disposal to maintain their privilege.

The justice gene is repeatedly aggravated when decisions are made for admission to top schools and professional programs. We talk of a meritocracy if we are admitted and a rigged system if we are not. Test standards and professional coaching for tests and essays tend to be the tools of the already privileged and unavailable or even unknown to those who do not run in the same privileged circles. These are real issues. However, for those who expect to be admitted, the sting of the wasp is a new experience, and they may go to great lengths to challenge the decision. For those who do not expect to be admitted, the sting of the wasp is familiar, and they may stop trying to avoid further pain because they already feel like they are living in a wasp's nest.

Although we do not have time to fully explore it here, it would be irresponsible to consider justice without considering mercy. Nick and Sarah may not have recognized it, but Frank offered them mercy without claiming it or demanding that they give him credit. In our unilateral quest for justice, we may forget the value of mercy whether in our homes, parking lots, or the justice system itself. Sometimes, our efforts to enforce our view of fairness allow us to forget context, kindness, compassion, and forgiveness, without which justice becomes nothing more than a rigid system of rules that denies the dignity of what it is to be human. No set of blindly enforced rules can fully embrace the richness of relationships individually and collectively. We must be wary of the rigid, instinctive rules that we unconsciously construct and apply.

Takeaway

The justice gene is binary—I'm right; you're wrong. Life and conflicts are nuanced and not binary, even though your mind, body, and soul will send binary signals. It is easier to think of pain as having a clear cause, effect, and response. But life is not like that. As your body gears up for a conflict, your justice gene will tell you that there is only one right way to experience and respond to the conflict—yours. You do not have to abandon your principles to think more broadly.

Action

When you feel the gut-wrenching physical symptoms of conflict, ask yourself if an immediate response is necessary. If not, let the other side go first so you can calm yourself. Listen, if you can, without preparing a response. You will likely think the other person is being unreasonable, but see if you can ask yourself why they *think* they are being reasonable. Every time you gravitate to how they "should" respond, you have stopped listening and are preparing to argue. It won't help.

5

Fear

Much like the justice gene, fear evokes a primal reaction, and it's not always a bad thing. Fear is essential for survival. But it can also stifle adventure, curiosity, imagination, and meaningful engagement with conflict. As with all primary emotions, it is not one single feeling, and it almost always runs with other emotions—even those that seem incompatible.

Someone once told me that fear and security or fear and faith cannot coexist. I say "beans" to that. Rather than being mutually exclusive, fear and faith or security exist on a continuum, with fear on one end and security or faith on the other. Add to this hope, which is the connector between the two ends that moves us more in one direction or the other. As I feel more hope, I gravitate toward security. As I feel less hope, I gravitate toward fear.

How does the fear-security continuum play out in conflict? Say I have a roommate who shares the rent with me, and she loses her job. I might be afraid that she won't be able to pay her share of the rent, and we will be evicted because I have no extra money. In that moment I'm likely feeling more afraid than secure. Hope might mitigate the fear as my roommate looks for jobs, I look for a second job, and we decide to call our landlord to ask for an extension.

But what happens if we agree on a range of options but disagree on which option is most promising or who is in the better position to take action? It is easy to overvalue our own efforts to resolve a conflict while at the same time undervaluing someone else's efforts. Our ideas about what is "fair" start influencing what goes on internally and externally. The conflicts in such a situation are many, and they are affected by how honest I am with my roommate about my fears and concerns and how candid she is about her responses, which are influenced by her fears about employment, money, and having a place to live. Then we get into the relational conflicts and how we balance supporting someone when they are down with caring about how they are responding to a financial crisis that affects the both of us. While hope influences whether we are tracking toward fear or security, the old saying "hope is not a plan" has some truth to it.

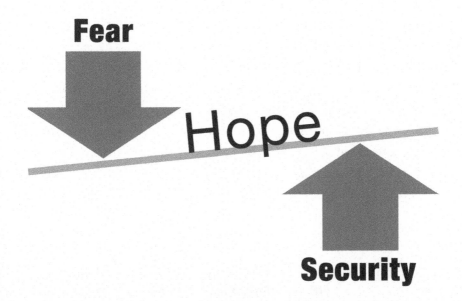

What Are We Afraid Of?

We praise our children for trying something hard and risking failure. However, the older we get, the less we tend to be willing to risk failing or losing. In fact, we are far more motivated by fear of losing what we have than we are by gaining something we don't have. The tradeoff calculator in our heads is running constantly, often without us knowing it.

Fear of losing could involve any of the four categories we are discussing: survival/security, affection/esteem, power/control, and comfort/ease.[1] They bear reviewing. Survival and security can be translated into fear of death, injury, and financial insecurity. Esteem and affection convert into fear of shame, embarrassment, or social isolation. Power and control become the fear of uncertainty, powerlessness, loss of mobility, and an unknown future. Comfort and ease are the loss of the moment of pleasantness or the introduction of uncertainty into a future that I thought was certain. You can add your own categories or describe them differently. These fears can manifest as low-level signs of discomfort or red-alert alarms that fully inflame every fiber of our being.

We also frame our discussions of fears based on their timelines. Fears that threaten our security or our self-esteem always live in future (uncertain) outcomes. Anxiety—another term for fear—about the future normally turns on *what if* questions. Fears about the future are always rooted in outcomes that are not completely within our control *and* the fact that we have decided that some of those outcomes are better than others. "What if I take this job and

---

1   Cynthia Bourgeault, *Centering Prayer and Inner Awakening* (Lanham, MD: Cowley Publications, 2004), 147. Again, Bourgeault does not identify these as fears, but as desires to let go of in a meditative practice. I added the last category, "comfort and ease."

then get offered a better one?" or "What if I commit to this relationship and then get dumped?"

Resentment about the past and the fear of what others might
think of us normally turn on *if only* statements. Things like "If only
I'd had more time to sleep, I would not have fallen asleep at the
wheel." These are rooted in the excuses for the paths we chose but
for which we do not want to be responsible. They cast us in the
light of the victim who lacked agency.

Our reaction to fear is similar to the way we feel an assault
to the justice gene. It is a full-body experience. Chemicals flood
our bodies, and we often react to the perceived threat before we
understand its degree. The way our minds and bodies react to different levels of threats can be so immediate that deciphering an appropriate response from a primal reaction can be difficult. Ideally,
our fear would be proportional to the magnitude of the threat, but
that would require us to have perfect foresight. For instance, the
fear of being embarrassed is very different from the fear of being
in a car accident, but our physical and emotional responses are the
same. Consider the child who hides behind the door and jumps out
to scare his mother. When the child jumps out and yells "BOO!"
there is no real threat to the mother, but her mind and body, working in concert, perceive a real threat, no different than if the child
were a burglar. She may quickly see the mistake, but it will still
require time for her heartrate to slow and for her blood pressure
to decrease.

Most daily fears lie somewhere between threats to our survival
and risks to our comfort. But at times we feel fear even if no actual
threat of danger exists. Regardless of whether the threat is real, if
we perceive fear, then the feeling is real. An acronym I once heard
is that fear is False Evidence Appearing Real. In these instances,
our fear is based on a construct, usually of our own creation, that
thrusts us into conflict with reality itself, only we don't know it.
The conflict becomes with the person or circumstance that we
perceive as the threat. It would be easy for me to say that the first

step in defusing conflict is to determine whether a fear is real or perceived, but that is way too easy. Rarely can we be talked out of our fear, even by those we most dearly trust. In reality, any fear we feel, no matter how groundless, becomes our reality.

Our upbringing, genetics, environment, and immediate situation influence our reactions to threats. Whatever our unique reactions are, if we are unable to recognize the fear and put it in context, it has the potential to consume us. A state of constant fear inflames our bodies and our minds and can lead to hypertension, heart disease, and mental illness, as well as other significant mental and physical health conditions. Therefore, in order to step into conflict, we must be willing to honestly embrace fear, which is far different than being fearless. And it is easier said than done.

Avoidance

Our fear can be so overwhelming that we will do everything in our power to avoid it. It is physically exhausting and emotionally draining, and at times we long for the comfort that avoidance can bring. This is not always bad. Sometimes we need to take a break from overwhelming fear to gather ourselves. However, avoidance is rarely a good long-term strategy, and it often creates the kind of isolation we are trying to avoid. And if we invest too much in avoidance, it can have unintended consequences. It can lead us to ignore potentially real and substantial threats to our person and our values.

One way we avoid facing or revealing that we're afraid is to say, "I'm fine." That one vague statement can reflect many possible truths. You may *be* fine; you may *think* you're fine (though in reality you are not); or you may *not* be fine but don't want to talk about it. Admitting to not being fine leaves us vulnerable.

"Fine" can be honest, or it can deflect attention. Often it is simply an empty sentiment to avoid thinking or talking about a situation that is not fine. So, when we aren't sure about outcomes, our private and public face defaults to "fine." Struggling in an unhappy marriage? "We're fine." Getting ready for a long drive on icy roads? "They're fine." Feeling a persistent and nagging pain in your chest? "I'm fine." Revenues not meeting expectations? "It's fine." We don't want a divorce. Or an accident. Or a heart condition. Or unemployment. So we tell ourselves and others that everything is "fine." For a time, saying we're fine might help us deal with uncertainty. And it might even be necessary to protect ourselves.

Sometimes it is not just that we lie to ourselves, but we also foist "fine" on others. It is easier to tell someone they're fine than to sit with them through not-so-fine circumstances for an indefinite period of time with no clear answers.

Another tactic we use to avoid fearful situations is to imagine a fantasy option. When the pain of the process of dealing with an experience that scares us is great, it's easy to fantasize that things will magically sort themselves out. She will change, and I will feel better with no conflict or effort on my part. Or, she will never change, and leaving this marriage will be an unqualified success. The truth lies somewhere between those options, and none of them happens without action on our part to invest in an uncertain outcome. It is the reality of uncertainty in conflict that sometimes reveals itself in apathy—another overlooked response to fear.

Sometimes my pride motivates me to avoid acknowledging that I'm afraid. That can be particularly true if admitting the fear makes me feel vulnerable about my inability to accomplish something I promised to do.

Patty is great at referring clients to our law firm. She is also compassionate, and she often refers people with difficult problems and no ability to pay. When these folks call, I always want to meet with them and help if I can. Sometimes the desire to help exceeds my ability, and I outrun my headlights. The conflict begins internally but expands externally, sometimes culminating in a humbling cry for help.

In one case, Patty referred a friend with a challenging and long-term issue that turned out to be full of legal complexities way out-side my skill set. I was familiar with the practice area but was not an expert. The case expanded to include multistate litigation, experts, and lots of money and risks. After accepting the case, I continued to plug away at it long after it was clear that I was overmatched. As a result, I was losing sleep and suffering from finger-tingling anxiety. Afraid to admit that I was in over my head and aware that the client could not pay, I told myself that I was doing "fine" and did not ask my partners for help. I was deeply conflicted between needing help and the fear of making myself vulnerable by asking for help. My partners had not volunteered for this pro bono project, and I did not want to ask them to bail me out.

Eventually, I sat down with two of my partners and told them about the ugly mess that I had made worse. I also shared that the client had no money. Without hesitation, my colleagues jumped in and lent their considerable legal expertise to the problem. The situation was ultimately resolved with more than twenty people involved in a dispute resolution process in another state. I was per-mitted to attend so long as I promised to be quiet. This conflict was settled in spite of me, not because of me.

Count the fears…I was afraid of losing the respect of the client. I was afraid of what my partners would think of me. I was afraid of asking for a favor from my partners who had not had an opportunity to be involved from the beginning. I was afraid of what Patty would think. So it pretty much hit all the fears from security to self-esteem to loss of control to discomfort. We touched all four bases.

Failures in the face of fear are not unique to people who are inexperienced. I was a lawyer with lots of experience. My desire to help was reasonable, but my fear interfered with good repre-sentation, and that was unacceptable. If someone with as much experience as I had was so hesitant to identify the problem and ask for help, it's no wonder that younger lawyers might be even less inclined than I was to get the help my client and I both needed. A good lesson for anyone who manages people!

Denial (It Ain't Just a River)

Avoiding fear can lead to the danger of fooling ourselves. That is when we step into denial. Just like we use *fine* to avoid feeling fear, we adopt various euphemisms that allow us to deny the vulnerability that comes with admitting we're afraid. Maybe you've found yourself deflecting fear by using a phrase similar to these:

» "I'm just stressed."

» "I'm not afraid of public speaking, I just don't like it."

» "I'm not afraid of telling Brad I love him, I'm just not sure I do."

» "I'm not afraid of telling Sarah I don't like her family, I'm just mad she even asked."

» "I'm not scared that my daughter won't make the right choices, just concerned."

» "I'm not afraid of what my wife will say, I just don't want the argument."

» "I'm not applying for the job because I don't care about it anyway."

So afraid we call it other things

You may have noted how frequently people use the word *just* to minimize fear. This is primarily because, regardless of any contributing factor, *just* defensively suggests that our response is reasonable and not out of proportion to the threat. Culturally, it is easier and safer for us to express discomfort or concern than fear. Fear is an admission of vulnerability. Words like *stress, dread, aversion, dislike, worry, concern,* and *anger* disguise what is fundamentally fear. There can also be an element of gender stereotyping at play in this. Our society has progressed somewhat, but many men may still feel that they are expected to be fearless. Angry? Sure. Frustrated? Definitely. But displaying the kind of vulnerability that comes along with admitting to fear can still be a risk depending on the context, the community, and the level of trust. Similarly, some women may be reluctant to admit their fear, especially if they feel it reinforces perceptions of weakness based on gender.

Paralyzed by fear of things I could not identify, I made one of the biggest decisions of my life. The outcome turned out well, but not because of any planning or insight on my part. I learned an enormously valuable lesson about fear, but it came with plenty of pain and took years to really internalize and understand it.

After an engaging and enjoyable four years getting a liberal arts degree in philosophy and religion, I was unsure what to do next. Others with similar degrees were going into various fields, from sales to management training to journalism to creative arts. I had no interest in any of those, but I also lacked an interest in anything else. A lack of passion or even curiosity left me feeling embarrassed by my own confusion.

At the time, law school was a reasonable extension of a liberal arts degree, whether one wished to practice law or not. In the 1980s, a law degree was also not an overwhelming expense. Nearly every law student, even without personal wealth, could graduate with manageable debt and find a job.

When I went to law school, I was prepared for the academic demands but unprepared for the commitment and competition necessary to do well. Friends and classmates studied hard, went to class, and committed to daily routines that enhanced their ability to flourish. I read and researched only as required and was undisciplined with my routine. I did not participate in class unless it was necessary. I often did not go to class. While my friends and classmates spent their nights studying, I watched reruns of the television show M*A*S*H, played my trumpet, and looked for any excuse to get out—going to a new movie, visiting friends, or hanging out at the local bar.

The first year of law school is the most rigorous. Good law schools make every effort to accept only qualified students, so failure is a pretty rare occurrence. However, the requirements of the first year often draw a sharp contrast between those who emerge as star students and those who finish near the bottom of the class.

After completing my first year and most of the second year of a three-year degree, I was in good academic standing but nowhere near the top of my class. My friends had distinguished themselves as outstanding students. I began to feel left behind. And no wonder. I did just enough to get by and excused my lack of effort as "just not interested." This profession of apathy was my unrecognized response to my fear of not measuring up. While my friends spent hours on end in an effort to excel without a guarantee that they would, I spent as little time as possible so I could have a built-in excuse for a mediocre transcript. Looking back, I see that I used many of those "just" euphemisms for denying my emotions.

Shortly before spring break of that second year and only four weeks from the end of the academic year, I was playing pool at the Pit Lounge. It was a local no-frills bar with a few low-hanging neon lights and cheap wooden tables and chairs. There were pool tables and booze. It reeked of stale beer but was a place that had come to feel like home.

Ron and I were classmates who gravitated toward each other and bonded over our dislike of law school and our attraction to diversions. On this particular Friday, as spring break began, most of our classmates had left town to be with friends or interview for jobs. Ron and I, believing ourselves to be romantic nonconformists, played pool and drank beer.

Ron wondered out loud, "What can we do to have some fun in the next week?"

We didn't have much money, but I tried to think of a road trip we might be able to afford if we pooled our resources. Ron didn't have a car, but I did.

"What if we drive overnight to Florida and watch the space shuttle take off?" I suggested. "Then we can drive to Edwards Air Force Base in Southern California and watch it land." I waited for Ron to confirm what a genius idea this was.

Instead, he looked at me skeptically. "How can we do that?"

"If we live on peanut butter sandwiches and beer and sleep in the car," I reasoned, "I think we'd have just enough money to cover gas."

Ron seemed to buy in. "We won't miss that many classes," he said finally. "And at least the year is almost over." We continued playing pool and complaining about our remarkably good lives. Like so many others, we weren't quite satisfied with what our privilege had afforded us: law school, decent grades, and the ease of life that comes with being young and insulated by the world of higher education.

Only much later, with the benefit of hindsight, could I see that I was far less happy than my reality would suggest. I would not have understood the concept of internal conflict if someone had held it on a bright yellow sign in front of me.

Ron went home that night and went to bed. I went home that night and stayed up convincing myself I was in such misery that the solution was not a road trip but a much more dramatic move: quitting law school and leaving town. Forget traveling to Florida and California to watch the space shuttle. Denial of my fear of failure required a much grander gesture.

Without talking to Ron, I got up the next morning and wrote

to the dean of students. I explained that I was quitting and spent two pages melodramatically justifying that decision. I've looked for my copy of the note, but mercifully I've been unable to locate it.

After I packed the next morning, I did not pause to ask anyone for a different perspective. I had friends and family who could have provided insight and support, but I asked for none of it. One class-mate and dear friend interrupted a business trip to Hawaii to talk me out of quitting. I answered the phone but did not listen and told him I'd talk to him some other time.

I did not consider the debt I had accepted to go to law school. I barely considered my two roommates and the rent I owed through the term of our lease. I thought only about how awful I felt, how deeply I had invested in my misery, and how quitting, no matter how ill-considered, was better than admitting to a fear I could not have seen.

There was not a single moment that I thought of my feelings as fear. I was unhappy. The unhappiness had been imposed on me, and any reasonable person in my position would also be unhap-py—this was the lie I sold myself. Leaving law school in the middle of the semester was all I could imagine. Denial illuminated the path to run away.

I sold my car, which gave me just enough money to pay my roommates for my rent and to buy a four-week pass on a Grey-hound bus headed west. I "ended" the relationship with my then-girlfriend, Patty, but I packed her picture and pined for her as I looked out the window of the bus. I sat at the back, drinking peach brandy with a couple of other sad passengers who, like me, were running from something but going nowhere.

The bus took me to Tucson, where I worked as a helper for a rural mailman to make enough money to move on. I crashed on the floor of a friend's apartment in San Francisco. Before my four-week pass expired, I landed in Lake Tahoe, Nevada, and got work in one of the casinos.

The manager of Harvey's Casino hired me as a barback, work-

ing 10:00 p.m. to 6:00 a.m. A beginning barback works in the bow-
els of the casino cutting lemons and limes, preparing the garnishes
the real bartenders need to top drinks for the gamblers. A barback
then graduates to the bar itself as the pourer for the cocktail servers. This involves holding a liquor gun in one hand and a mixer gun
in the other. The servers call out the drinks, and the barback mixes
them in the glasses as fast as possible on a tray so the servers can
get the drinks to the customers quickly. I was horrible at it, and the
servers, who depended on tips for their livelihood, were constantly
angry as I poured the wrong drinks into the wrong glasses.

As I settled into this new life, uncomfortable, ashamed, and
In less than four weeks, I had gone from a passing law student
to a failing barback. I lived in the back room of a house owned by
an old man who could just make ends meet by renting his two
spare bedrooms to me and a failed minor league baseball player
turned gas station attendant. Though these two men's lives were
difficult, they were both much happier with their existence than I
was with mine.

As I settled into this new life, uncomfortable, ashamed, and
feeling like I'd been backed into a corner, a letter arrived from the
dean of the law school. This letter, a beacon of hope in the darkness
of my circumstances, changed everything. Rather than point out
my irresponsibility, he noted that I had apparently considered this
move for a long time. He was sorry we had not talked about it. It
did not occur to me that he had talked to many students who had
felt like me over the years. (I thought I was terminally unique.) He
withdrew me from my classes so that I would not automatically
fail. Since I was in good academic standing, except for cutting and
running, he said that he would give me a one-year leave of absence
to return to law school with no requirement to reapply.

He finished his letter with: "The unexamined life is not worth
living."

I had not expected a reprieve or even thought I needed one. I
was so thoroughly invested in the denial of my true feelings (fear)
that needing a reprieve was never on my radar. I'd have owned up

to sadness, depression, and maybe even irresponsibility and selfishness, but I still would not have recognized the fear that compelled me to leave. I was missing Patty and unable to succeed as a barback, and the letter was a ray of hope.

My panicked decision to run away rather than alleviating my unhappiness aggravated all my fears: fears of losing safety, self-esteem, connection, and comfort. I may have had options A, B, or C to choose from for dealing with my situation, but every one of them would have required some kind of self-reflection and pain. For me, the only choice was option F—fantasy. Option F was running away with the expectation that a pain-free resolution to my conflict would magically sprinkle down on me.

Ron, meanwhile, graduated from law school as planned and moved to Washington, DC, where he worked for a congressman and then managed a small local bookstore that grew into a nationally known independent juggernaut. I'm not sure if he ever got to see the space shuttle.

I also graduated from law school. I married Patty and got a job as a lawyer in my hometown. However, it would be years before I faced the issues and the thinking that led me to quit school. Patty, our three daughters, and others who knew me paid a price. I was good at investing deeply in how I felt and bad at honestly reflecting on myself and accepting responsibility. Recognizing fear and conflict, asking for help, and taking suggestions from others was a slow and painful process that took years.

If someone had asked me in the days after I quit school about my decision, I'd have repeated the fantasy in my head that I could have done as well as the other students if I had worked as hard as they did. That, of course, is total fiction. First, we will never know how I would have compared to my classmates because I refused to put in the necessary effort to find out. Second, it was far easier to make the excuse of minimal effort, employing the vocabulary of denial, than to put in the work and risk realizing that I wasn't as talented or smart as they were. Rather than hazard doing my best and falling short, I created an entire narrative that *justified* running away. Sometimes our biggest fear is finding out we don't measure up. Some of us would rather stay on the sidelines than risk falling down. There is nothing wrong with that decision, so long as we make it with clear eyes and we own it.

I was fortunate that Dean Fromm threw out a lifeline that gave me an opportunity for a redo. The detour I took will not be in anyone's handbook of how to face fear. With the benefit of time and a willingness to listen to the wisdom of others, my response to fear is different now—at least on my best days.

Fight, Flee, or Freeze

When we do actually feel the fear, the natural responses are to fight, flee, or freeze. The best option? That depends on the circumstances. And the degree to which we react depends on how much time—and presence of mind—we have to evaluate the situation.

In some situations, fear provides a jolt of energy in the form of anger, which usually feels empowering. Anger is routinely an expression of fear, as we saw it was to unfairness, and it often triggers and fuels the fight response. It does not have to be an objectively big fear for us to get angry in response to it. If being on time to a meeting with clients is important to me and my partner picks me up late to get there, I will get angry. My body and words will reflect anger, and I might start a fight by saying, "You know how important this is. How could you be late?" The anger, however, is a response to the basic fear of losing esteem or affection. It may also be the fear of losing security and survival if the meeting is essential to securing a big piece of business.

More fundamentally, if you see a child about to run into the street, you may hear a mother yell loudly and angrily from the front porch, "Stop! Right now! Don't move!" as she runs toward the child. If you watched her body language without access to the context or the words being spoken, it might be difficult to see the difference between fear and anger. The context and words reveal that the anger is an expression of her fear.

For some of us, any action in the face of fear—even the wrong one—feels better than no action. We may take immediate steps to do something because it allows us, whether we're right or wrong, to believe that we have control in that moment. But acting impulsively in response to fear usually happens at the expense of making an informed decision. We give up the power to thoughtfully choose in order to feel the power of acting. Unfortunately, our impulses do not typically lead to a rational, logical, well-thought-out approach to managing conflict. A rational, logical approach is not devoid of emotions such as fear or imagination but factors them into the decision. Even during those times when we pause to consider the options, we will need to resist the impulse that feels the easiest to act on in the moment, although we don't want to thoughtlessly discard it.

Becca graduated from college with a degree in informatics and was offered several prestigious consulting jobs. A mentor/professor who had been very encouraging to Becca suggested that she might want to indulge her entrepreneurial spirit and accept a job with a start-up instead of with a big consulting group. A start-up backed by a famous tech celebrity had also offered Becca a job. Becca did not feel any draw to being an entrepreneur, but she wanted to please her professor, so she gave the offer from the start-up serious consideration. Becca did not feel a sudden onset of fear about making a decision, but she did feel the vague discomfort of making a decision that offered no circumstantial guarantee of the correct outcome. She did not know the future, and she could not predict her "best" choice.

Becca hated making decisions. She was plenty smart, but she always felt pressure to make the best decision based on some artificial benchmark that she couldn't quite articulate. These kinds of fears confront us in all sorts of circumstances, but they feel more like a low-grade fever than a gut-clenching panic. In such situations, we have more time to reflect on our motivations and perhaps seek help to be honest with ourselves. Becca wanted the security of a good job. She wanted the esteem of her professor, but she also wanted the chance to be trained by an internationally respected organization. She wanted the power to control her destiny, but at most she could influence it, not control it. Comfort and ease were nowhere on her chart.

Becca made a T-chart of the pros and cons of both job offers and talked to her older sister, Chloe, about it. Chloe was a painter and had no interest in doing any of the things that interested Becca, but she had great interest in Becca herself. Becca presented the chart to Chloe, which counterbalanced the adventure of independent learning with the dependability of well-established training and experimental work with fixed assignments. The chart did not give Becca any more clarity. The anxiety was becoming great enough that she considered going to graduate school just to avoid deciding. That was her decision-making version of a flight response to fear.

Chloe then made a suggestion. "Maybe this can't be reduced to an equation. Either choice is good if you decide it is." This is wisdom that is always easy to offer but always harder to live by.

"Why don't you close your eyes and imagine every detail of going to work at either job," Chloe continued. "Picture getting ready in the morning, driving to work, entering the office building, seeing your coworkers, going to lunch with friends, and doing things on weekends."

Chloe paused. She hadn't mentioned anything about the actual work.

"Tell me about how that makes you feel at either place," Chloe finished.

Becca said nothing for a long time, and then she smiled.

"Guess I'm going to be an entrepreneur," she said, breathing more easily.

Fear can make us feel an urgency to decide quickly. If an immediate decision is not required, then sitting with the fear and imagining the details of what a choice would look like can soften the fear and allow for some clarity to emerge. This can be true with relationships, work, retirement, and buying homes.

Acceptance

As we've seen, fear can own us without our knowledge. Taking any action, even unhelpful action, creates the illusion of power when we feel uncertain and powerless. But such actions often leave us feeling vulnerable and still unable to identify what we're really feeling. We will feel discomfort, experience conflict, and cause more pain for ourselves and others if we choose to deny or run from our fears or lash out in anger in response to them.

Making thoughtful choices when confronted with fear requires us to accept some degree of discomfort and invest in patience as we await an outcome. We can neither predict the future outcomes with certainty nor know for sure which one will be better. We are constant oddsmakers in our heads.

We also value perseverance in the face of uncertain outcomes, but we mostly value it and respect others for persevering *after* we or they experience a good outcome. If we persevere and "lose," we wonder if we've wasted our effort. We might even shame the person who persevered and did not objectively "succeed" for making a bad choice, being a failure, or being stupid. Because we know this, our brains are constantly processing perceived risks based on the fear of being shamed or ridiculed.

Those who deal with fear well accept that there are a number of possible results, and while they may prefer one over another, they can be OK, whichever one happens. A friend told me the story of a saxophone player who lived alone in a small efficiency apartment in South Bend, Indiana. The saxophone player was very talented, and big bands routinely invited him to leave his small apartment and travel an hour to Chicago to play with them. He played with some of the best musicians of his era, and other musicians marveled at his talent.

One of the bands got a longstanding gig in New Orleans, and they invited him to join them. They had a train ticket for him and a place for him to stay. It would be more money than he had ever made, but he said no.

"Why not?" the bandleader asked.

"If I stay in my apartment in South Bend, I can think I'm the best saxophone player in the world," he said. "If I come to New Orleans, I have to find out."

That might not have been the best choice this person made, but at least he made it fully aware of his fear and without deflecting it with avoidance or covering it up with denial.

It is crucial to remember that the relationship between our level of fear and the responses it evokes are nuanced. Our fear response is as individual as we are, influenced heavily by our emotions, background, previous experiences, self-awareness, and ability to communicate. It also depends heavily on our comfort level in dealing with some pretty hefty emotions. That's when our fight, flight, or freeze reaction kicks into gear—when we feel compelled to stand our ground, or run, or hide and hope the threat goes away. But embracing fear, especially when we can convince ourselves to take a step back before reacting on impulse, can help us navigate conflict and reduce the chances of making things worse.

Takeaway

Fear is a powerful driver in all conflict, and acknowledging it can allow us to make good choices about whether to engage or not engage in the conflict.

Action

The next time you recognize that there is a conflict between you and someone else, see if you can identify what categories of fear might lead you to engage or not. Ask yourself if you're afraid of losing:

» Security and survival

» Esteem and affection

» Power and control

» Comfort and ease

6

Power

Power is the ability to control circumstances, things, and people—including ourselves. When we feel injustice or unfairness and when we are afraid, we seek power to create a feeling of security and control. Sometimes it is real. Sometimes it is illusory. If we regain a sense of having power, we may feel relief, but by itself and without perspective, the relief is as transient as taking an aspirin to temporarily treat a chronic backache. So in reality, power is our perception of control, and our perception of how we exercise power may or may not be accurate. The same can be said of our ability to predict the consequences of exercising power.

People can disagree about what we mean by power. If power is only about domination, then the physically, financially, or emotionally strongest person will likely get their way in the short run. But power does not have to be overwhelming or dominant to have impact. Influence of any kind is power. If we couch power more creatively, then it is how we wield influence that pushes us toward the more or less powerful end of the continuum.

Power is too complex to fully cover in this chapter, but it is important to be aware that it drives conflict by conveniently reducing every conflict to an exclusive power-versus-power dynamic. Without an awareness of the many glaring and subtle ways power steers our conflicts, such as by distorting our perceptions of the cost of exercising power or misperceiving who has it, we become unwilling to add to our kit of tools to engage with conflict.

Absence of Power

If power is the ability to exercise control over circumstances, things, and people, then we would be wise to realize where we or others lack power. Poverty often feels like the absence of power, and I tended to think of it exclusively in terms of financial poverty until I read a book called *A Framework for Understanding Poverty*[1] by Ruby K. Payne, PhD, an expert on poverty and education.

Payne speaks to ways in which people (particularly children and students) are impoverished, which is the opposite of having power. Her definition of poverty is "the extent to which an individual does without resources."[2] When I read her summary of different kinds of impoverishment, it was clear that it was not limited to children and students and that we are all impoverished in some way to varying degrees.

She highlights eight different kinds of resources that leave people impoverished:

1. *Financial.* Having the money to purchase goods and services.

2. *Emotional.* Being able to choose and control emotional responses, particularly to negative situations, without engaging in self-destructive behavior. This is an internal resource and shows itself through stamina, perseverance, and choices.

---

1 Ruby K. Payne, *A Framework for Understanding Poverty*, 4th revised ed. (Highlands, TX: aha Process, Inc., 2005).
2 Payne, *Framework*, 7.

3. *Mental.* Having the mental abilities and acquired skills (reading, writing, computing) to deal with daily life.

4. *Spiritual.* Believing in divine purpose and guidance.

5. *Physical.* Having physical health and mobility.

6. *Support systems.* Having friends, family, and backup resources available to access in times of need. These are external resources.

7. *Relationships / role models.* Having frequent access to an adult or adults who are appropriate, who are nurturing to the child, and who do not engage in self-destructive behavior.

8. *Knowledge of hidden rules.* Knowing the unspoken cues and habits of a group.[3]

The fact that we have an abundance of one kind of resource does not mean that we are not impoverished in other ways, and perhaps that abundance blinds us to our lack of resources when defined as broadly as Payne describes them.

The Sports Jacket

Our experiences and the groups or circles in which we live may leave us blind to our own impoverishment or protect us against our poverty. The fact that we fit in with one group does not mean we fit in with other groups. I remember going to a party wearing a brown polyester sports jacket when I was a freshman in college. The jacket looked fine to me. I was talking to a female classmate who came from an affluent family in a large city. Most of the people at the party were from similar backgrounds. I was from a small farm community.

3　Payne, *Framework*, 7.

"I love it that you're wearing that," she said, pointing to my jacket.

At first, I thought she was complimenting my jacket, but then I realized she saw how out of place my clothes looked. The men around me were all wearing dark navy worsted wool blazers. I had not noticed the difference until she made the comment.

In a split second, I had to figure out what she meant. She was complimenting me—but on my willingness not to fit in, not on the jacket itself. She thought I knew the hidden rules of how to dress in this social clique. She thought I was an iconoclast. She had no idea that I thought I *did* fit in. Although my face flushed with embarrassment, I went along as if of course I was doing it as a joke. It was blind luck that I understood the context before I thanked her for liking my jacket and before I became defensive about not knowing the rules. I don't think she was being unkind. She thought I was in on the joke and that I had in fact instigated it.

The power in that circumstance was not a matter of life, death, or money, but it was a matter of power, or rather impoverishment, in social currency. I did not understand the hidden rules, but I was learning them quickly. And the power of the lesson is with me forty years later.

The Social Research Subject

While the previous story is an example of being blind to our own impoverishment, this is an example of being blind to the impoverishment of others—others who are well aware of their own impoverishment. After the midterm elections of 2018, I heard a person from a family that has been impoverished in many ways for generations talking with a young social scientist doing field research.

The discussion was a heated one about social benefits.

"You don't have any idea what our family has suffered at the hands of people like you," Wendy said to Caleb, the social researcher.

"Well, let's at least have a civil conversation about it," Caleb responded uncomfortably.

"Civil conversation!" Wendy replied. "You want it to be civil just so you can control what I say and keep me in my place. You can't tell me how to talk."

The conversation ended there.

By asking Wendy to be "civil," Caleb was imposing his own rules of civil discourse as if they were universally applicable. He missed an unspoken rule of Wendy's group: "Take no s---." Additionally, Wendy's family suffered from financial insecurity that has created physical, emotional, and other shortfalls that impacted her family's entire world. Caleb was asking her to respond with the same emotional detachment *he* felt to issues that profoundly affected *her*. It was his implicit version of "set aside your emotions and be rational"—never a good tactic.

Although he might not have said it, Caleb assumed he had power by virtue of his education and privilege, and he tried to exercise it by telling Wendy how she needed to have the conversation. While Wendy had the ability to speak in a way that would have made Caleb comfortable, she was tired of being left behind and then being told—by people who knew very little about her day-to-day struggles—how she should express her feelings about it. She sensed that Caleb's imposing his rules on the conversation meant that he perceived her as less important than him. Wendy made it clear, by expressing her outrage in her own way, that Caleb, as the interviewer, did not have the power to control her. By refusing to do what someone in perceived authority asks or requires of us, it shifts the anxiety to the one who mistakenly believes that they possess all the control. Wendy did more than cause pain; she exercised her own power by saying no to Caleb's.

Caleb had no idea that what he considered "civil conversation" could be an act of privilege used to oppress someone who made him uncomfortable. Further, if Wendy had yielded to his need for polite discourse, it would have kept him from hearing what pain someone else was experiencing in her own words.

The point here is not whether Caleb's way of communicating

should have been seen by Wendy as oppressive. The point is that Wendy *did* see it that way. Caleb probably had no ill intent, but his benign intent was insufficient to send a message of partnership with Wendy and resulted in her feeling disrespected. If Caleb wants to communicate more effectively with people who come from different backgrounds, then he will need to develop broader tools. He can start by listening more, not jumping immediately into his agenda, and caring about the people he is interviewing. By acting as if he unilaterally had the power to control the interview, he diminished whatever positive influence he had.

One way Caleb might have salvaged the conversation would be to start with an apology instead of a scold about civil conversation. He could have asked Wendy for her help, with the admission that she had every right to refuse. He could have been humble enough to say that he was trying to understand problems, not aggravate them, and admit that he just failed miserably. He could have begun by thanking Wendy for participating and telling her that she could stop any time and say what she wanted as she wanted. He could have invited Wendy to tell him if he was screwing it up. Wendy would get to be the authority on how or whether the conversation continued. By giving Wendy the power to control not only her answers but how the conversation unfolded, Caleb would be giving up the perceived power of his own agenda and surrendering to hers. Surrendering to Wendy's way of conducting the conversation would show that he was secure enough not to need power. This approach is incredibly effective and totally counterintuitive.

Recognized and Unrecognized Power

Whether we believe we have great power or little power, it is easy to become defensive when our power is challenged. We tell ourselves stories to make sense of our circumstances. We are human, and if these stories leave us feeling vulnerable or threatened, we may justify extreme behaviors in response to our fear of losing power. Proportionate power responses are difficult to summon in the face of extreme fear. If we find ourselves feeling invincible and completely in control, or feeling so hopeless that we want to exact a price on someone else, then seeking counsel from someone we trust to test the feeling and the response is important.

In conflict, it is always important to consider alternatives to exploiting the power you have or to fighting to gain power you don't have. The alternative might be to surrender to the other person's agenda, to explore possibilities for working through the conflict, or to abandon engagement and then decide whether to come back later. Here are two stories. One reflects a thoughtful use of power and the other reflects how tragic outcomes can result when we misgauge the pain of someone who feels powerlessness.

CEO *vs Little People*

In a pitched battle between a large company and several of its customers, I represented a senior executive with lots of power who showed a deep understanding of when and when not to use it.

Customers of the company sued because they felt they had been badly mistreated. The company did not think they had mistreated the customers. The litigation had been going on for years. As with most conflicts, legal or otherwise, no one is likely to convince the other side they are wrong. The customers and their lawyers had been very effective in getting their story into the press before I was involved. I represented the company in a specific case, and a judge ordered us to mediation. On the day of the mediation, I met my client at the airport.

He got in the car and asked, "What's my job today?"

"Is your goal still to settle this lawsuit?"

"Yes," he answered. "We don't think we did anything wrong, but the publicity sucks and we'd like to be done."

"If you want to finish," I said, "then your job is to sit there and take it."

"What do you mean," he asked, a little irritated.

"Whether you think you did something wrong or not, these customers feel like they have suffered enormously, and they blame you." I began. "These folks are already righteous and angry. If you offer a weak apology or defend or explain what the company did, you will do nothing but aggravate their righteous anger. Angry, righteous, and defensive people do not normally make good decisions."

He was willing to listen, so I continued.

"They have an excellent lawyer, who is willing to try this case. You are in a position to listen to them instead of making them listen to you. They will expect you to be arrogant and condescending. You can change the tone by hearing them without interruption and by making no excuses. You have enough money to offer in settlement that it should make sense for them to at least consider it if you don't insult them first."

People with financial power can endure drawn-out financial conflict, but the less common and wiser ones consider whether it is worth it.

The mediator invited the other lawyer to tell us why she thought my client owed her clients a lot of money. I don't remember all that she said, but I remember how she ended.

"You and your company should be ashamed of yourselves. It is not just the company but how you personally behaved," she said looking my client in the eye. "At every step of the way you could have stopped this, but instead you stepped on all the little people, with no regard for the impact on their families. You just hoped that no one would take their case, and you were wrong," she said with a glare.

My client took it.

When she finished, the mediator turned to me to respond. I felt my own heart rate increase as I prepared to respond. Before I could say anything, my client looked at me and waved me off. He was going to speak before me.

"Thank you for being so candid about the way you and your clients feel," he said, looking directly at the lawyer for the customers

and then at the customers themselves. "It is clear that you have suffered. We may not agree on everything, but I don't want to insult
you by having my lawyer tell you how we see things differently.
We are here today to take an honest shot at settling this case, and
I hope we can." He looked at me, making it clear that I was to say
nothing.

When I said he needed to sit there and take it, I didn't mean
that I would be mute. However, it was his case and his risk. His
response was as unusual as it was brilliant.

He made not a single argument to counter the lawyer's claims,
although he believed there were many. He made no admission of
wrongdoing. But he did not minimize the pain that the customers
felt. My client stated quite honestly that he wanted to settle the
case if he could.

He represented a company that could easily afford to continue
the litigation. Even if they lost on every claim, the company would
not be financially threatened. Once he decided to settle, however,
legal defenses would have done nothing but robbed the customers
of a face-saving way to settle the case. Without saying anything
about "principles," he was willing to let the customers have theirs
without challenging them. It was a remarkable display of setting
aside power.

The case later settled for a number that made sense for everyone.

This was a wise executive. The powerful have a greater ability
to live in comfort and deny the universal fears of loss of security,
esteem, and control that are regular companions for those without
the power. He had power but chose to use influence. His ego was
not vested in winning; it was vested in ending litigation and getting
on to the more productive parts of his job, even though the lawyer
personally insulted him. He actually redefined what it was to win.
It was not to squeeze the last nickel out of the customers on the
other side. It was to settle the case for a number that was worth it
to him and his company. By not inviting a power struggle, he put

the customers in a position to hear offers and talk to their lawyer without the added overlay of anger that might have arisen if they'd felt disrespected.

Loss of Power Leads to Tragedy

Sometimes we see power imposed in ways that leave people feeling hopeless. When people feel hopeless, oppressed, and powerless, they may take extreme measures because they see no other alternative. The decision-making becomes binary—surrender and die or inflict as much pain as possible before death (literally or figuratively). Keep in mind that the suicide bomber made a choice that seemed to him or her to be the most reasonable among the alternatives they could imagine. We are incapable of interpreting with certainty how and why people make choices in the middle of conflict, or how they will respond when it is apparently resolved. For example, when couples get divorced, the unpredictable feelings that influence the decision-making process and the balance of power are very difficult to evaluate.

When a relationship goes bad, partners have conflicting notions of justice, vulnerability, uncertainty, mistrust, and fear of future consequences. That very same relationship that is about to end likely began with feelings of warmth, generosity, love, and visions of a future together. The collision between what was expected and what has happened leads people to feel powerless.

One or both spouses search for power as their lives spin out of control. Whatever control either one felt within the marriage is turned upside down. Formerly predictable behavior is no longer predictable. Sometimes the spin stops at a mediation, sometimes with a judge's decision, and sometimes the spinning, fueled by fear, does not end.

I will not forget my last divorce mediation.

The phone rang on my desk about six o'clock on a Friday evening in August of 2002.

"I'm a reporter from WTHR news. Is this Sam Ardery?"

"Yes," I replied hesitantly, being unaccustomed to calls from television reporters.

"Did you mediate the divorce between Jeff and Rose?" she asked.

"If the court record says I mediated it, then I did. If not, then I didn't. I can't say any more about it. Why do you ask?"

"According to the police, Rose killed her boyfriend, his ten-year-old son, and her own ex-husband," the reporter answered.

There was a long pause.

"I'm very sorry," I said mechanically and with disbelief. "I have nothing else to say."

We hung up.

I do not remember what happened in the mediation, nor would I be able to share details. I can say that Jeff and Rose were represented by respected and experienced lawyers. I can also say that the mediation ended without a settlement. Their divorce was tried by a judge who made decisions about how the marital property would be divided, who would have custody of their very young son, and how much child support would be paid.

It was weeks later that I got the call from the TV reporter.

One good friend, after going through her divorce, said, "I think we are all mentally ill when going through the trauma of a divorce."

A few months after the murders, I ran into Rose's lawyer on the street. She had as much experience and as good a reputation as any family lawyer I knew. I asked her about the case.

"If you had lined up one thousand of my clients," she said, "I'd have picked her as the least likely to ever do something like this."

I just shook my head sadly, and we walked on to our different destinations.

This may not seem like a story of fear or power, but I think it is a story of both. I say that with no inside information personally or legally about Jeff or Rose. I have no idea what, if any, diagnoses Rose may have had, or what her immediate response was after the judge issued the terms of the divorce. But I believe to the depths of my soul that when we are taxed beyond what our resources allow us to bear, others may very well not see it, and primal fear leads to a grasp for power stronger than nearly anything we can imagine. A feeling of powerlessness combined with righteousness can justify almost any behavior we can imagine.

When it comes to conflict, we experience our own internal conflicts and then use our experience and reasoning to either engage or run from the conflicts with people and circumstances outside ourselves. Our instinctive notions of fairness and justice can get violated, and we fear a future that is out of our control. If we experience primary fears of losing security and survival, esteem and affection, power and control, and comfort and ease, it can feel like the world has descended and is suffocating us. We can crumple under the weight of the fear of everything we hold dear, or we can look for power—a natural desire to regain some agency. This is not a time when our best thinking emerges.

If we are without sufficient financial, emotional, family, social, or mental health resources to support us in a time of despair, then power that would otherwise seem unreasonable starts to make sense. For reasons I do not know and cannot diagnose, the power choice that made sense to Rose was to kill three people. And no one in the chain of her relationships—personal or professional—expected it.

Most of us have not made the choice that Rose made, but nearly all of us have felt the finger-tingling anxiety of fear that led us to consider alternatives that would have seemed unthinkable in a different state of mind.

This true story is not to criticize people who knew her and wished they had seen this coming. It is to illustrate that regardless of income, social standing, education, race, or religion, we are imperfect predictors of the behavior of others (and sometimes ourselves) when it comes to the extent that we will chase power to offset our fear. We need to be aware of it in ourselves and in others. The common sense we so deeply trust can miss essential clues.

Side Effects Abound

Not long ago I talked to someone who is an executive in the pharmaceutical industry. He said, "One hundred percent of the drugs we develop to treat a disease have a side effect. Some are more dangerous than others, but they all have one." Power is like a drug to relieve the pain of fear. And like drugs, there is nearly always an unintended side effect.

When we fight power with power, the most predictable short-term consequence is that the one with the most immediate power wins the current struggle. Power that is blind to its unintended costs raises the risks to everyone in the sphere of influence. If we are in the group that does *not* have much power, we experience risks to our safety and security. Those with power do not like discomfort any more than those without it, and they may fail to foresee the consequences of wielding their power.

United Airlines Wants a Seat

On April 9, 2017, United Airlines flight 3411 from Chicago to Louisville was full. The airline needed to transport a crew to Louisville, Kentucky, but every single seat was taken. United had gone through its normal voluntary procedure to open seats, but they still needed a spot. The airline staff then asked a passenger who also needed to get to Louisville to surrender his seat. Feeling fully within his rights, he refused to get off the plane.

United and security officials decided to forcibly remove the passenger from the plane. The violent removal and the reaction of fellow passengers was captured on video.[4] The man, obviously in

---

4   Julia Jacobo and Cameron Harrison, "Doctor dragged off United Airlines flight after watching viral video of himself: 'I just cried.'" *ABC News*, April 9, 2019, https://abcnews.go.com/US/doctor-dragged-off-united-airlines-flight-watching-viral/story?id=62250271.

great physical and emotional distress, was dragged screaming from the plane with a bloody nose.

Let's consider how this happened.

The person bought a ticket for the flight. He walked through security at the airport. At the gate, he showed his ticket to the United Airlines boarding agent, was checked in, and took his seat.

What most of us do not know is that a "contract of carriage" is included when we purchase an airline ticket. The airlines are permitted to overbook flights, and if there are not enough seats, they have a legal right to require passengers to give their seat to another flyer. The airlines are supposed to have a procedure to do this and to explain to passengers what that procedure is.

So, up to this point, the man, a paid passenger, behaved legally and appropriately in taking his seat. United Airlines behaved legally in requiring him to involuntarily abandon his seat.

Both sides appear to be right. The passenger, a medical doctor, was worried about getting back to Louisville to treat patients the next day. United was worried about not getting a crew to Louisville to make another scheduled flight.

This is a classic example of what happens when power and fear of losing power collide. The basest way to resolve conflict is with physical force. United made that choice. The passenger made the choice to resist, and security officers forcibly removed and injured him. When conflict is "resolved" by power against power, there is always a winner and a loser. And sometimes everyone loses.

Neither party—at least to start—was out of line. Both were justified in their very real belief about their rights and their worries about the possible impact of missing the flight or delaying the crew. The passenger had every reason to believe he had a right to keep the seat he paid for and checked in on time for. United had every right to believe that it could enforce the rules that the passenger (likely unknowingly) agreed to when the airline sold him the ticket.

We can parse the law, the rules, and the regulations, but ultimately, conflicting entitlements collided. Neither party deferred to the other. The party with superior power enforced a solution, and both sides underestimated the consequences. The video reflects the passenger's efforts to enforce his rights based on his fear of losing his power to get home as planned. But those consequences would not have happened had United not enforced its response to its fear of not getting its crew to Louisville. By exercising their legal rights, United resorted to maintaining power through violence.

It was reported that the security guards broke the passenger's nose in the scuffle. When the viral video began to make the rounds, the CEO of United at first publicly defended the airline's decision. The passenger hired a lawyer. Social media blew up with criticism, primarily aimed at United.

In the end, the passenger is reported to have confidentially settled his grievance with the airline. The other passengers on the plane were allegedly given vouchers to compensate for the anxiety and discomfort of the ugly situation. The CEO did not get good public reviews.

United might not be seen in the best light here, but consider the trauma to the frontline employees. They were likely given little or no discretion. The rules assume compliance by passengers. They were told by supervisors to get the passenger off the plane. We saw the result when it turned out that the only way to do that was to physically remove him. Although it was the job of security to remove the doctor, their own adrenaline was likely rushing when the dispute became physical. There was no one in this scenario who stepped back to reconsider. When we think we are right, we are rarely creative enough to quickly change course. We literally cannot imagine an alternative path or the consequences we may face if we're wrong.

From the passenger to the security personnel to the United CEO, each person involved was doing what they thought was reasonable and legal. They all believed they were acting within their rights. So, let's assume they all were. What good did it do anyone who thought they were right? The passenger ended up with a settlement, but not before being physically and emotionally damaged. And the CEO kept his job and defended his company, but perhaps at the expense of his career's projected path.

When the response to conflict is raw power, unintended and very often unpleasant results are likely. The side with the most power will likely win the immediate battle, but future consequences are uncertain and often underrated. The passenger and United both invested in their righteousness to defend their power, and both underestimated the price they would pay. Everyone was hurt, including the passengers who had to watch it. I'll say it again: being right is really expensive and way overrated.

Both the passenger and the United Airlines employees had alternatives, but all were unwaveringly committed to their rights. Once it became clear that the airline was going to use physical force, it was a time for one or both sides to pause. This was not a case of illegal or inappropriate behavior. It was a case of convenience and enforcing rules.

When the power player chooses to enforce rules by using physical force, it is time to stop. When a person is having force imposed on him, it is time to stop. Both sides can then consider whether convenience for either of them should come at the cost of imposing or resisting physical force. For it to have ended differently, one or the other would have needed to surrender their righteous anger. However, giving up our rights when we don't fully understand the consequences is a very difficult path to take. In addition, there are times when rules are routinely and wrongly enforced, and positive change requires someone paying the price to stand up for themselves to effectuate change. It helps when the conflict is captured on video and shared around the world…depending on which side you are on.

Out of Our Hands

Power is the perception of control. We are drawn to power over powerlessness, but there is an ever-present danger of failing to recognize the pitfalls of recklessly wielding power. Our instinctive draw to power when we're afraid often clouds our judgment, making it difficult to see the impact we're having on those around us. It can also lead us to believe we have power we don't.

Few things can make us feel as powerless as watching a loved one struggle with something we can't control. Powerlessness becomes profoundly personal. For my family, this became evident in August of 2018.

Patty and I had just returned home after being out of town, when Patty's phone showed a call from our middle daughter, Grace.

"That lump on my leg," Grace said, "it's cancer."

"Oh no," we both said without knowing what else to say.

"Are you sure?" we asked.

"Who are you seeing?" we continued without pausing for an answer.

"Who is your doctor? What hospital? What comes next?" we went on without pausing and mindlessly seeking information.

"Your questions are not helping," Grace said. "I'll let you know when I have more information."

We stayed on the phone a bit longer, but not much.

At the time of Grace's diagnosis, she lived in Chicago, home to some of the best cancer treatment centers in the world. Although her cancer was rare, she was not the only person suffering from it. Three large Chicago-area hospitals had specialized medical teams to treat her kind of synovial sarcoma.

Grace called in a couple of days; we tried to stuff our questions that were natural but served no one but us. We were afraid and must have thought that information would give us power.

"I can't get in to see the doctor for two weeks," Grace said in a flat and depressed voice. "Do you know anyone who can get me in sooner?"

"We'll start making calls," I said without waiting for Patty to respond.

My mind raced with people we knew who might be able to help—doctors, lawyers, educators, hospital administrators, friends who had been treated for cancer in Chicago. Any remote acquaintance felt like fair game for my intrusive calls. My idea of an emergency gave me an entitlement to contact anyone I could reach at any time. If they did not call me back right away, I called again...and again.

There may be a universe where this is OK, but not the one in which I used my fear to rationalize all my calls. I knew I had no power over Grace's cancer, but if I had the power to influence any part of it that made Grace less anxious, then I was going to do it.

"Hello, Dr. Smith," I said to a doctor in another city who was an acquaintance of an acquaintance, "My name is Sam Ardery and I was given your name by a mutual friend."

Before I went on, he said, "Tell me again how I know you? Do you know it is ten o'clock at night?"

"I'm sorry," I said, "but my daughter has cancer and..."

He was very polite, but he knew what I ignored—lots of fathers' daughters have cancer. They all want the best treatment immediately.

"I can make a call," he said, "but the best thing would be for Grace to make her own call to get in sooner. There is nothing quite like a patient advocating for herself."

Virtually the same conversation happened many times over with all sorts of people. I wheedled and argued and debated and negotiated. I learned—not for the first time—that power struggles do not bring out the best in me. I also learned that I rarely have as much power as I hope, nor am I as good a negotiator as I believe.

My behavior exposed my lack of resources in my present state. The powerlessness felt like a dark kind of poverty that I did not know how to deal with. If we tick down Ruby Payne's list of resources that people suffer without, we can name several—emotional, mental, and spiritual. My fear could justify almost any response that had a chance to further my agenda, and I was unable to hear suggestions until my own efforts fell flat.

In the end, my calls and interruptions made no difference. Grace and her husband, Chad, did all the heavy lifting for Grace to get the care she needed in the time that the doctors were able to provide it. However, if I could have done anything to move up the time period, I would have done it. In my scared state of mind, my irritating and selfish efforts almost seemed noble to me.

Only in retrospect could I consider the potential price to other people's children, spouses, parents, and siblings. Although there is no indication that my actions moved up any of Grace's appointments or treatments, if I'd had a direct or indirect way to do it, I would have. Not once did I think about the consequences of responding to my fear with my effort to exert power. What if someone else's appointment had been moved back because Grace's had been moved up? What if I could have persuaded someone to move Grace to the front of the line and bump someone else out of it? What might the consequence be to the person who was seen later or by a different doctor? What if something had happened to one of them because of my actions? How was I entitled to transfer my fears to the next parent whose child and whose fears were just as important as my own? In this case, my poverty was my selfishness and thinking that in some way my family was more special than other families. My entitlement blinded me to the poverty of my selfishness and the potential cost to others.

When I am not overcome with fear of uncertainty, I will readily admit that the suffering of my own family is no more important than that of another's. But in that moment of fear, I never even thought of it. I chased that illusion of power. Because it involved something life-threatening, I could justify it in my head.

Chasing control in response to the fear of the unknown is seductive and sometimes dangerous. My response to my fear for Grace did not end up with me shooting someone, but I would not be shocked if the parts of my brain responding to my fear of a lack of control might have been very similar to Rose's when she made a decision to shoot three people. When we are consumed with fear and searching for a powerful antidote, it is a time to be circumspect, which does not come naturally.

Decisions that seem justified in a sustained moment of terror routinely miss the mark when examined with the benefit of hindsight. We are all brilliant looking backwards. There are many times when our attraction to using power is decidedly not benign.

Takeaway

Power does not always declare itself in obvious ways, but chasing control is a natural, if not always helpful, response to fear, powerlessness, and poverty.

Action

The next time you feel anxiety, stress, or discomfort in response to a circumstance or a person who disagrees with you, stop and consider whether you could be OK if you exerted no control but did something differently from what you prefer. Things might not turn out the way you had hoped, but there is a different kind of power in learning that you are OK, even when the outcome is not the one you designed.

7

Bias and Stereotype

B*ias* is that person, place, or thing that I prefer over another. I may prefer warm weather to cold weather, funny people to morose people, savory to sweet, sedentary to active, or blue to yellow. More dangerously, I may prefer people who look, think, and act like me to the exclusion of many, or possibly all, others. By itself, bias is neither good nor bad. However, bias affects our choices, our relationships, and our conflicts. There would be no conflicts if we all had the same biases—we would all prefer and agree to equitably share the same things in the same way.

We don't all prefer and agree to equitably share the same things. And biases can quickly turn into entitlements when we feel threatened. The way we choose to navigate our biases, privileges, and power perpetuates inequities that drive intractable conflict.

Stereotyping is the efficient way we categorize information. It is the shortcut our brains take to make quick decisions and to avoid evaluating and reevaluating every circumstance as if it were new to us. Stereotyping works by drawing inferences from the general to the specific and from the specific to the general. An example of drawing an inference from the general to the specific is thinking that because every person I've met from Colorado loves hiking, Matilda from Colorado must love hiking. An example of drawing an inference from the specific to the general is thinking that since my pit bull is cuddly and friendly, all pit bulls are cuddly and friendly.

We stereotype things because it takes less energy to draw conclusions when information is neatly categorized. That's why when we are confronted by exceptions to our stereotypes, it's easier to write them off as outliers than it is to have our brains do the work of sorting out every unique situation. However, the efficiency that drives stereotypes creates assumptions that might not only be wrong but can also be unfair and aggravate conflict. Efficiency and fairness are frequently in conflict.

In this chapter, we will talk about some stories that reveal areas where our biases and stereotypes become evident. I am at a loss to describe any conflict where either a bias or a stereotype is not relevant, and we are barely skimming the surface of a topic deep with research and consequences. However, to consider conflict without touching on bias and stereotype would be a big miss.

Seeing Bias in the Mirror

If your first instinct is to deny your biases and willingness to stereotype, you're not alone. Most of us would like to think of ourselves as tolerant, impartial, and reasonable. But in reality, our biases and the stereotypes we hold about other people are often ingrained so deeply that we are unconscious of how they influence how we think and behave. A belief in one's own biases and stereotypes is universal to all human beings.

Before we dive into some specific examples of how our biases and stereotyping affect conflict, you can test yourself. When driving and someone cuts you off in traffic at the merge point, have you ever looked at the driver of the offending car, seen that they were a different race or gender or age or appearance than you, and then had a negative thought about them, not just about their driving but about their race, gender, age, or appearance? Did you put this person in a particular category? It is not a good thing to have this reaction toward an anonymous driver we'll never see again, but it's far more dangerous when our biases and stereotyping influence who we hire, give opportunities to, or fill the ranks of the military, police, and other security organizations with.

If the driving test doesn't convince you and you'd like to prove me wrong (or prove yourself right), you can take an Implicit Association Test online.[1] The test, designed by Mahzarin R. Banaji and Anthony G. Greenwald, is structured to challenge and measure our instinctive tendency to stereotype. It tests our preferences regarding race, gender, age, weight, and other areas in which we might have conscious or unconscious biases. The two professors have literally written the book on the subject of implicit bias.[2]

In their book *Blindspot*, Banaji and Greenwald note that a person can possess a bias without endorsing it. For example, we can have a bias based on a stereotype of old people but then consciously choose not to endorse it or base our behavior on it. That choice becomes harder when we are dealing with dire consequences. When the stakes are higher, our ability to suppress our prejudice and make unbiased decisions is challenged. Often, we fail.

To illustrate the tension that exists between conscious and unconscious bias, let's consider a single systemic stereotype that became a life-or-death issue for many unborn babies in the 1940s and continued through most of the 1970s. In the face of powerful medical evidence, doctors ignored science and risked the health of unborn children.[3]

---

1   Project Implicit, Harvard University, 2011, https://implicit.harvard.edu/implicit/.

2   Mahzarin R. Banaji and Anthony G. Greenwald, *Blindspot: Hidden Biases of Good People* (New York: Bantam Books, 2016).

3   Margaret Heffernan, *Willful Blindness: Why We Ignore the Obvious at Our Peril* (New York: Bloomsbury, 2011), 45–46.

Alice Stewart was an English medical doctor who began practicing in the 1940s. She was qualified, highly trained, and respected
by her peers. Dr. Stewart was also young, divorced, and the mother
of two small children. Because World War II was well underway
and women could not be drafted, she had greater freedom and access to information than many of her female predecessors had. Her
natural interest, experience, and ability to analyze data made her an
early expert in the field of social medicine and epidemiology. These
two disciplines deal with facts that reflect the impact of practices
and behaviors on the health of people. The studies can include
the consequences of exposure to toxins in a workplace, the effects
of smoking, or the impact of X-rays taken of pregnant women.
Dr. Stewart noticed some correlations between X-rays on pregnant
women and the later health of their children.

Reporter Margaret Heffernan tells the story of Dr. Stewart in
gripping detail. Stewart began an extensive study of what might
contribute to childhood leukemia and resultant deaths. Her study
revealed that if a child's mother was X-rayed while pregnant, the
child was twice as likely to develop cancer and die. Other medical
professionals, including some in England's medical community, reviewed and supported Stewart's results.

The study's causal link between X-rays and health risks to unborn children was published in major global medical journals in
1956 and 1958.[4] And yet it took over twenty years, until 1980,
for American medical experts to recommend against performing
X-rays on pregnant women. Great Britain did not follow suit until
a year later, in 1981.[5]

Why was so much of Stewart's theory and research ignored? In
the mid-twentieth century, X-ray technology was relatively new
and touted as a harmless, noninvasive diagnostic tool. The medi-

---

4   Heffernan, *Willful Blindness*, 49.
5   Heffernan, *Willful Blindness*, 48.

cal community believed in its efficacy, and they hoped the general public would do the same. Starting a panic over the risks involved with X-raying pregnant women would have been a bad look for the medical field. And the medical establishment was made up overwhelmingly of men. Additionally, Stewart was young, divorced, and a woman—a triple whammy when it came to biases and stereotypes men of her generation and in her profession held about women. She was also working in the field of epidemiology, which was fairly new and not well understood. Her male counterparts had their own motives, agendas, and perceptions about Stewart's findings and pushed back against them.[6]

Sadly, the bias of the medical establishment against someone so unlike them led them to ignore facts. Who knows how many babies could have been saved if the facts had been allowed to speak for themselves?

Though the consequences of our own personal biases and the stereotypes we hold may not be quite so dire, our unfounded confidence in our conclusions and our dismissive attitudes toward anyone who challenges those conclusions can still have a far-reaching and damaging impact. We need to pay particular attention when we think about ignoring a conflicting opinion and our reason for doing so is based solely on who voiced the opinion.

No One Is Smarter Than We Are

There is nothing quite like unyielding confidence in our own judgment to reinforce biases and stereotypes. And our single biggest bias is in favor of ourselves. Francesca Gino is a professor at Harvard University who has studied bias. She's used scientific rigor to reflect what I have seen anecdotally in my professional and personal life: we have an overwhelming bias toward our own thinking.

---

6   Heffernan, *Willful Blindness*, 50.

Dr. Gino has delved into how we make decisions by analyzing real-life situations.[7] She talks about game show participants, bankers, and retail executives suffering from the same tendency to discount outside advice. In each case, the decision-makers had access to outside information to inform how they would make important decisions. Each one of them defaulted to their own conclusions instead of heeding the advice of people whose opinions they had requested and even paid for.

The game show contestants played a game of chance. They chose from among various boxes, which had big prizes, small prizes, or no prizes at all. At various junctures, they could stop and keep what they had or go forward and try for more, but only if they were willing to risk losing everything. They could rely on their own instincts or consult the studio audience. After analyzing four hundred decisions, two tendencies emerged. First, the players tended to ignore the advice of the audience. Second, if they had followed the advice of the audience, it would, on average, have increased their earnings.

A banker Gino discusses, Richard Syron, was the CEO of the mortgage lender Freddie Mac in the years leading up to the financial crisis of 2008. According to a 2008 *New York Times* story, Syron's chief risk officer warned him in 2004, four years before the crisis, that underwriting standards had slipped in a way that created risk to the company and the country. Others also allegedly issued similar warnings. Syron ignored the advice of his risk expert and criticized the *New York Times* story. The result was that shareholders lost billions. The US Treasury put Freddie Mac into receivership in the fall of 2008. Syron lost his job.[8]

The retailer Walmart was already wildly successful by 2006

---

7 Francesca Gino, *Sidetracked: Why Our Decisions Get Derailed, and How We Can Stick to the Plan* (Boston: Harvard Business Review Press, 2013), 18–20.

8 Gino, *Sidetracked*, 20–21.

when the company decided to enter the German market. Gino recounts that Walmart CEO H. Lee Scott and other Walmart executives consulted German retail experts for their opinions about opening in Germany. The German managers offered advice on German laws and culture. The Walmart decision-makers ignored the insights from the German experts in favor of their own instincts. Walmart's initial foray into Germany failed.[9]

Gino's findings were painfully similar regardless of whether the decision-maker was a game show contestant, a banker, or a retail executive: decision-makers routinely ignored outside advice. How counterintuitive then for any of us to act contrary to the biases and stereotypes that we have been reinforcing for a lifetime.

Gino found four commonalities among the contestants, the banker, and the executive. First, they had access to outside information. Second, that outside information conflicted with their own conclusions. Third, when outside advice conflicted with their instincts, they went with their instincts. Finally, had they relied on the outside information, the results usually would have been better.

When it comes to *why* we ignore advice from outsiders, Gino suggests two possibilities: One is that it's difficult or even impossible to determine whether the advice is good or bad. The other, which is more compelling to her, is that we struggle with listening to the advice of others, no matter what we have paid them, when we have expended significant effort on reaching our own conclusions.[10] Because we have spent a lot of time thinking about it, and because we have great common sense or instincts, conclusions that conflict with our own seem not as good. Rather than thinking that the time we have spent is a sunk cost, for better or worse, we use it as a seal of approval on the conclusions we have reached, frequently to our detriment.

---

9   Gino, *Sidetracked*, 21–22.
10 Gino, *Sidetracked*, 22.

Gino's exclusive focus was not on conflict, but she identifies a huge driver of ongoing conflict: our innate bias toward our own ideas. The mistake we make is to think that all we do know is all we can know.[11] And we act accordingly. In this mindset, we commit to the conclusions we have already reached and look for the data that support them. Our biases and stereotypes become more entrenched. Working to overcome our biases and stereotypes requires a choice to practice that which is uncomfortable. Just as it is easier to sit on the couch at night eating cookies and watching TV than it is to exercise or finish homework, it is easier to justify our own thinking than it is to be open to the possibility that we might be wrong.

In the sixteenth century, the French writer Michel de Montaigne said, "I consider myself an average person, except for the fact that I consider myself an average person."

Montaigne said it; Gino proved it; we all live it.

Smarter than My Old Dad ... Maybe Not

As we've seen, we will find reasons to justify our opinions, beliefs, and ways of doing things. This applies to how we consider people around us. We often fill in their stories and attach qualities of thought, behavior, and value to them that are consistent with stereotypes that have little basis in fact. We quickly reach conclusions about someone's morality, intellect, interior life, and judgment. We draw conclusions about other people in a split second. These conclusions then get run through our biases, and we favor or disfavor someone or their opinions based on what we already prefer and the categories we have conveniently assigned to them. No matter how unfair, inaccurate, or reprehensible our conclusions

---

11   Michael Pollan, *The Omnivore's Dilemma: A Natural History of Four Meals* (New York: Penguin Books, 2006), 180.

might be, we will defend them almost before we have thought them. Sometimes our defense feels harmless, but other times it can have significant impacts that we miss.

My dad and mom lived in the same home that our family had moved into when my brother and I were in high school. My mom was eight years younger than my dad, and as they aged, my brother and I would frequently stop by to check on them. If you want to experience conflict in real time, try telling an aging parent what he or she can't do.

One late November when I paid such a visit, I pulled into the driveway and saw my ninety-year-old dad at the top of an extension ladder getting leaves out of the gutter as my petite eighty-two-year-old mother tried to stabilize the ladder at the bottom.

"What in the hell are you doing?" I yelled at them, opening the door of the car almost before it stopped.

"What do you think?" my dad responded, turning toward me and making his position even more precarious.

Watching his response reminded me that my own reaction was not well considered. I walked over to where they were standing and sidled up next to my mom to hold the ladder.

"We're not cleaning out all the gutters," she said, supporting the decision she and Dad had made to do this themselves. "We're just getting a couple of spots that seemed clogged. We thought we'd be done before you got here."

At that moment Dad tossed down a clump of wet leaves that landed partially on my head. I don't think it was an accident.

"Is that it?" I asked, hoping he really was done.

"I'm coming down. Hold the ladder steady," he instructed, as if I were less capable than my mom, who was half my size.

He came unsteadily down the ladder with his replaced hip, cortisone-injected knees, and disabled shoulder. We went inside.

"You know that's crazy," I said as we sat down at the square kitchen table of my childhood.

"Are you saying that old people can't still do things?" my dad asked.

"You know I'm not saying that," I said. "But falling off a ladder and finishing your days in a nursing home or dying is not a good risk to take."

"So now you get to decide what risks are OK for us, huh?"

"All I'm saying is that people younger and healthier than you get hurt on ladders, and cleaning out your gutters yourself is a bad idea," I answered, not wanting to have the battle about my parents' autonomy.

"Do you think we're thinking OK?" he asked.

"Except for getting on extension ladders, yes," I said, getting in a dig.

"Is every ninety-year-old the same?" he asked next.

"No."

"Is every fifty-seven-year old the same," he asked next, referring to my own age.

"Obviously not," I said.

"Are the gutters clean, and are your mom and I sitting here at the table with you?"

I didn't answer.

"You think you're so smart, but you don't know what it is to be ninety," he said. "You put all old people into one big group. Are you sure that you aren't more afraid of how you'd feel or what you might have to do if I did fall than you're worried about your mom and me? You take risks every day and so do we. You make your decisions and we make ours. As long as we aren't hurting anyone else, we get to decide. But thanks."

Conversation over.

He was right about much of it, and I still wonder if my fears weren't about me as much as they were about them, though I could rationalize otherwise.

Recounting the conversation makes it sound more contentious

than it was. My dad was a gentle man, but he was also a stubborn man. I had decided that I knew what was best for him. I had stereotyped him not just as an old man—he was—but as a man whose age meant that he had to stop doing certain things.

My parents' mental health and the joy they got from their lives were partially a by-product of their continuing to do as much for themselves as possible. Some of those things included risks. Most people would agree that some of what they did was risky. However, by putting them in a box, I was trying to keep them safe at the expense of some of the meaning they still found in their lives.

This was not a conversation about driving and taking away keys because other drivers and pedestrians were at risk. It was a conversation about limiting the activities of a ninety-year-old man and his eighty-two-year-old wife who were thinking just fine. He and my mom were not oblivious to the risks; they were simply willing to take some risks. Did my stereotype of what "old people" should do and my fear of the consequences give me a right to control their behavior? They didn't think so, and over time, I came to agree.

My parents continued to live their lives in that same home until my dad died four years later. In the summer, Mom would prop him up on the rototiller so he could balance himself on the machine while she held him up from behind by his belt. They would tell me about it afterward, and we all laughed at the silly but joyful picture of their labors.

Stereotypes don't have to be about protected classes or people we don't know. Our deep confidence in our own thinking about those closest to us can be distinctly unhelpful with those we think we know best. The combination of stereotyping, righteous thinking, and the perception of control can cause conflicts right in our own backyards. For every stereotype that applies, there is an exception.

The Untrusted Advisor

When you add bias and stereotyping to the natural preference we have for those who are like us, our associations and friendships become uniform and lacking in diversity, creativity, generosity, and compassion. In theory, difference sounds great; in practice it is messy and uncomfortable. The result is that we can almost always rationalize preferring people who are similar to us in one or more ways. People's ability to be biased in favor of their in-group is endless. We make the rules for ourselves and others, but we apply them selectively. By investing in biases and stereotypes, those who might claim to practice a rigid moral code can find ways to make exceptions to their code. Those exceptions can include what we disclose or don't disclose to people who are trying to help us.

I was part of a team of lawyers representing one side of a very expensive and contentious business breakup. Our client, who was from South America, was enormously successful in the jewelry business in the country where he was born. Because of political unrest there, he decided to move his family and businesses to the United States. He found a naturalized American citizen to be his business partner and help with the transition. Our client entrusted this person to move assets, buy property, and coordinate the move. His new partner was originally from the same country as our client, and they shared a faith tradition.

A serious dispute arose between the two men. They hired lawyers and filed numerous claims and counterclaims against each other. After a series of depositions, something just did not make sense. I was sitting in a conference room when my senior partner felt that he needed to confront our client.

"Julian," my partner said, "you've said over and over again that you've told us everything, but something is missing. The way you and Rex are fighting doesn't add up."

Julian just sat there staring as my partner's voice rose and he began yelling. Finally, Julian spoke.

"Listen," Julian said, matching my partner's tone, "I may be fighting with Rex, but he and I grew up in the same country and believe in the same God. You are a white American lawyer, and you do not really know what it is to be me or what I believe. There is no way I could trust you with all the information."

So, this very sophisticated businessperson felt more tied to the person he was litigating against than to the lawyer he was paying tens of thousands of dollars to help him. The bias and stereotype that came out in one sentence was true on its face. His lawyer was white; Julian was not. His lawyer was American; Julian was not. His lawyer grew up one way; Julian grew up another. His lawyer believed one thing about God; Julian believed something else.

Engaging with, listening to, or being open-minded about other people or ideas can be seen as a betrayal of our group identity. It can leave us vulnerable to being thrown out of our group while at the same time perhaps not being deemed trustworthy enough to be admitted into a new group. Openness to outside ideas threatens our security, our self-esteem, our survival, and our comfort and ease. We can criticize biases and stereotypes as character flaws, but to set them aside is a courageous choice, without guarantee of a safe place to settle.

Even in the middle of high-stakes litigation, Julian's biases and stereotypes left him trusting the person who he claimed took his money. Although he felt cheated by Rex, he trusted him more than the person from another culture whom he'd hired to help justice prevail. Conflict, indeed. Julian had no one to fully trust, and he felt like he was choosing between two untrustworthy options.

Value of Getting the Whole Story

Differences as small as the way we speak expose biases and stereotypes that create conflicts in what seem to be benign circumstances. In the last chapter, we discussed Wendy, the economically disadvantaged participant in a social research study, and Caleb, a young social sciences researcher. The two did not discuss race, religion, or gender in that encounter. But the wording of the research questions exposed biases and stereotypical thinking that made it difficult for Wendy and Caleb to communicate and not be defensive.

When I mediate, nothing seems benign. Whatever the issue, it has become big enough that people have given up resolving the situation on their own and have hired lawyers. They come to my office often after years of litigation that sends people to their separate corners full of anger and resentment. Sometimes lawyers help, and sometimes we get in the way.

Lawyers called me to mediate a case where a woman of color, Donna, had been released from a rigorous training program that she had worked years to qualify for. She was one of a few women and the only person of color in the program. After she was released, she hired a lawyer and sued the program. Nerves were so raw on all sides, including with the lawyers, that no one planned to be in the same room when they came to my office to mediate.

Donna and her lawyer asked me to begin in the other room, and so I did.

"We wanted her to succeed," Harrison, the program manager, told me when I entered the room. "I put my reputation on the line. In fact, we so wanted her to succeed that we hired a mentor devoted exclusively to her to ensure her success. Donna missed tutoring sessions, ignored the mentor, and underperformed at every level."

"Did you meet with her before she was released?" I asked.

"Briefly. She cried for about twenty minutes without saying much, and left," he answered. "I reviewed all the evaluations and talked to the mentor. I had to be objective and not swayed by emotion."

We talked far more extensively, and then I went down the hall to talk with Donna and her lawyer.

Before I could say anything, Donna began.

"I'm so embarrassed. I've never sued anyone. I worked incredibly hard to get into this program. I pride myself on my independence, and when I went in to talk with the director, I started sobbing and couldn't defend myself," she said with frustration. "I was determined to make it on my own, but they treated me from the beginning like I was different. No one else had a mentor. No one else was getting special attention. I knew I was different because I'm a woman of color. They treated me like I was incapable of making it without special help. My classmates didn't think I was one of them, so I had no friends in the program."

Donna had more to say.

"In the middle of all this, my daughter got sick. I was missing scheduled meetings. I was so short on money that my phone was periodically turned off, and I lost calls and confused schedules. Since they already seemed like they had an eye on me, I didn't tell anyone about my daughter or my financial struggles. I didn't want to be the 'special' woman who couldn't make it without help."

She stopped talking for a long time, looking down at the table.

"Then I became the woman of color who failed," she said. "I'm devastated."

We all sat silently in the room for a long time. It seemed like a circumstance where money would not be a good fix.

"Do you have any interest in sharing that story with Harrison?" I asked.

"We need some time to talk without you," Donna's lawyer said before Donna could answer.

Nearly an hour passed before I was invited back into the room. Now the lawyer talked.

"I don't think I've ever done this," Donna's lawyer said, "but if Harrison is willing to meet only with Donna and with no one else in the room, she'd like to have that conversation."

I went back down the hall and talked to Harrison and his lawyer.

"Donna has suggested that she meet with you alone, Harrison," I said. "This isn't standard operating procedure, so my guess is you need to talk with your lawyer."

They both nodded, and I left the room.

Another hour passed, and Harrison's lawyer came out to see me, without Harrison.

"What's going on?" he asked. "Are they just looking for a novel way to create more liability for us? This whole idea makes me uncomfortable."

Trial lawyers are fancy risk evaluators. We consider what our clients want. We weigh conflicting stories. We look at alternatives, we speculate about odds, and then we give advice. There are so many variables that we chase control like it's the holy grail. These lawyers didn't even want to be in the same room with each other. The idea that they would completely abandon control to let highly agitated clients be in a room alone is far outside the box.

"All I can tell you is what I observed," I answered. "They kicked me out of their room as long as you did before allowing me to bring this idea to you and Harrison. Donna seems sincere about wanting to talk with Harrison alone. If you or Harrison think it's dangerous, then don't do it."

Both sides decided to allow Donna and Harrison to meet privately.

There is no easy way for institutions and programs that have been steeped in traditions that have systemically excluded people to easily resolve those issues. There is no easy way for those who have been excluded to feel like the institutions have done enough. When those who have been privileged talk with those who have been excluded, they hear things very differently. Emotions understandably run high, and efforts to reach out on either side can seem inadequate and insincere. As I make these broad-stroke statements with my own conclusions, I'm stereotyping the privileged and the excluded.

For those competing for limited positions in elite programs, there is always someone who feels mistreated for not being accepted. When someone likely to be admitted in a previous process is denied, they feel mistreated. There is no program administrator, whether it is of an elite college, medical school, or prized internship, who has a universally embraced approach.

Individuals who like the idea of inclusiveness often feel differently when they get looked over for a coveted spot. It is always easier to let others pay the price for systemic change than to pay it ourselves.

People who have been traditionally left out because of race, gender, or religion may get in and feel like they are treated differently from others, as if they "only got in because..." They may have these feelings even if there are no facts to support them. If they get help to succeed, the presumption that they needed it is insulting. There can be a feeling of isolation and lack of belonging.

Finally, when the presenting issue appears to be one of bias and stereotyping, then it is easy to presume that it is the only issue. Any problem from the perspective of either side is easy to categorize as a diversity issue. That puts a complex problem into an impossibly simple container. Once we focus on diversity and inclusion issues, all things seem to return there, which is far too simple for the complexity of human interaction.

I was not in the room when Donna and Harrison talked alone. All I know is what was reported to me.

Harrison had no idea that Donna felt like a bright light of "less-than" was pointed at her by having a mentor assigned to her. Donna had no idea just how much Harrison wanted her to succeed. Donna thought Harrison believed she could not succeed without assistance. Harrison thought the mentor was to protect against potential problems because this was new, not because Donna was not capable. Harrison thought he was being polite when he did not follow up on the conversation in which Donna was too upset to speak. Harrison thought he was reaching an "objectively" supportable decision when he relied on evaluations and conversations with the mentor to release Donna from the program. Donna thought Harrison was one more man of privilege in power who had no interest in following up with her after she was so distraught in his office. They spent an hour and a half by themselves while the other lawyers and I anxiously bit our fingernails.

It was impossible for Harrison or Donna, either one, to say how much of their responses were driven by any bias or stereotyping, but those concerns existed in the background. They were both experienced and sophisticated communicators. Neither was likely to overtly talk about, or necessarily even be fully aware of, their biases and prejudices. We just know that they had them.

Without lawyers or a mediator, Harrison and Donna worked out a way for Donna to return to the program, which she successfully completed. She no longer had an assigned mentor, but she had Harrison's cell number to call if issues arose. Donna did not need to call for help, but she continued to stay in touch with Harrison about issues surrounding the successful inclusion of people who had been overlooked in the program.

We will talk later about trust, but there was something in both Donna and Harrison that allowed them to step outside the box of categories and to set aside lawyers to speak directly with each other. They had a conversation that they could not have had without the courage to step boldly into conflict.

In the short run, thoughtlessly investing in our biases and stereotypes is easy, comfortable, pleasant, and efficient. Our brain's quest for comfort has an enormous capacity to ignore hard evidence that conflicts with our closely held beliefs. Conflict is uncomfortable, and comfort is alluring. To relieve discomfort, we let go of one conflicting story so that we can invest in the other. As we ignore the conflicting information, that choice literally acts as a painkiller. It gives us the illusion of control and allows us to deny uncertainty. We tell others facts that support our views, but we are likely to ignore facts that don't. This natural but ineffective approach leaves no space to engage important challenges to our conclusions. Bias and stereotyping remove nuance, claim righteousness, cast blame, deflect responsibility, and reinforce what we believe without testing it. Donna and Harrison stepped out of the safe box of avoidance and burned it to have an uncomfortable but honest conversation.

Discomfort is inescapable if we are going to choose something other than our biases and stereotypes. These choices ignite fundamental fears of insecurity, isolation, and embarrassment or shame. In a polarized social and political climate, we treat biases as if they are expressions of unassailable clarity and stereotypes as if they are sacred insights. That binary approach of right and wrong leaves no place for positive conflict.

Takeaway

Biases and stereotypes are deeply embedded, and we may be unaware of them. Anytime our preferences are challenged and we become defensive, listening rather than rebutting is a path to learning and possible positive change.

Action

The next time you find yourself angry with another driver, see if you attach any negative biases or stereotypes to that person. Do you want to rationalize them away as if they don't matter? Think how those biases or stereotypes might be damaging in other areas of your life.

8

Trust

When I am struggling to have difficult conversations in a mediation, I will sometimes say to people, "You have no obligation to trust me, but if you are unwilling to trust me, then you should fire me." It sounds extreme, but if we cannot trust the person we have hired to help us, whether it is a doctor, psychologist, accountant, or car mechanic, then we had better find help elsewhere.

Ultimately, we *choose* to trust people as much as we require that they *earn* our trust. That goes against our common perceptions, countering what we tell our children, friends, and coworkers: that trust must be earned. But I believe it down to my bone marrow. People get to behave however they wish, and we get to *decide* whether to trust them—both before they have "earned" it and after they have "violated" it. Then the questions become: Who do we *choose* to trust? And why? Can we both trust and not trust the same person, and even ourselves?

Trust is a risk, but our personal, social, and professional lives would be stifled without it. And so we make the choice to trust a family member, friend, or coworker, with very little evidence, because not to trust them creates ill will and strains our relationships. No one in our lives behaves completely consistently all the time, and it just plain makes our brains work harder to evaluate inconsistent information. Here again, we often unconsciously rely on our bias that favors our own good thinking. We think that since we made the decision to trust, it is probably a good one. But we can do it incrementally and test trust on smaller things before we go all-in. It does not have to be all or nothing.

Who We Choose to Trust

To engage conflict well, we have to own our biases and prejudices when it comes to trust. As I discussed in the previous chapter, we tend to trust people who look like us, think like us, or are somehow connected to us. We often give the people who belong to our cultural, educational, financial, and religious groups breaks that we don't give to those who don't belong. We go so far as to allocate two strikes against some people before they even get to the plate and advance others to third base right away. Some we will never trust because we have already decided that a particular difference between them and us makes them untrustworthy. But if we are aware and practice some skills, we can creatively and thoughtfully broaden our willingness to trust. Once again, this is an invitation into discomfort.

In addition to trusting people who are similar to us, we also tend to trust people based on their credentials. We assume that the bus driver, whom we have never met, has a driver's license and the requisite experience to safely deliver us to our destination. We also tend to trust doctors, lawyers, accountants, and pilots without knowing them. We *choose* to trust them. Rarely do we actually *check* their credentials. When was the last time you asked to see the doctor's diploma or the pilot's flight certificate before being examined or getting on the plane?

Perhaps you disagree with my premise. You might say trust has to be earned and re-earned. If that is so, then how do you explain our decision to let a sixteen-year-old drive a car? Sixteen-year-olds don't have fully developed executive thinking. Teenagers are more prone to engaging in impulsive behavior and making bad choices. Yet we give them the keys to our cars and let them drive off alone, even if our knees are quaking a bit as we do so. We may even let them drive after they have an accident. Just as important, we get on the road knowing that *other* people's sixteen-year-old drivers are randomly driving toward us.

Why do we choose to trust inexperienced drivers? Because it lightens our load. It is a trade-off we make between fear of harm and comfort of lifestyle. We *choose* to gain time back from carpooling and from waiting in the parking lot after every volleyball practice or band rehearsal. This is an example where trust and mistrust collide, and the tradeoffs are real. We trust that we will be safe on the roads even though we mistrust some of the drivers who are also on the road. We hope that the risks are low enough that we will not be in the percentage of people who are at the wrong place at the wrong time when the sixteen-year-old driver makes the mistake.

Add to that our personal biases: we think our children are the "good kids," not the "irresponsible" kids other people have. Other people's kids are the ones who cause the accidents, not our own children. I have mediated too many wrongful death cases involving teenaged drivers, and none of their parents expected the tragic result. Still, I continued to let my own teenagers drive with the hope, but not the assurance, that the same thing would not happen to them. It is dangerous in any situation to think we are the exceptions, but we do it daily.

This is a good time to consider the tension between trust and mistrust. Perhaps they coexist, as they do when we consider our teenaged driver.

Mistrust

Most of us have areas of our lives where we mistrust ourselves. For some of us, that means not buying potato chips because we know if they're in the house, we'll eat the whole bag at once. Almost all of us have money taken out of our paycheck for retirement and health insurance rather than counting on ourselves to write a separate check. We'll tell a friend about our commitment to have a difficult conversation with our boss so that we have accountability. These are all things we do because we don't fully trust our own behavior.

Mistrust is not limited to the choices we make regarding our own behavior. We see it in institutions and workplaces. The boss micromanages the employee because of fear of outcomes. The employee does not tell the boss of a looming problem because of fear of the boss's displeasure or loss of the job. We forget that by not trusting others, their loyalty to us also erodes. And when we find ourselves routinely mistrusted, our loyalty to the person, group, or company that mistrusts us deteriorates. This fear-based mistrust erodes relationships and organizations.

The Bar-Coded Office

Peggy worked in risk management at a very large international corporation. She had been at the company since graduating from college. The company put her through graduate school and offered benefits that paid for her children to go to college. Peggy liked her job and felt valued by her employer. She became head of risk management when she was five years away from retirement.

Peggy supervised more than a hundred employees and had a well-appointed corner office. One day, a person with a handheld computer and bar-code stickers came unannounced into her office. He said that he'd been instructed to attach a bar-code sticker to everything in the space with the exception of personal clothing and paper products. This included the desk, chair, coat rack, lamps, file cabinets, bookshelves, and even pens. He wasn't at liberty to rifle through her desk, but everything on or around it was fair game. He told Peggy that he and a team of employees were doing this in every office in every location in the company "to prevent theft."

Peggy asked him, "Is there a theft problem?"

"I don't know," he answered, continuing to take inventory.

Peggy and her colleagues routinely handled hundreds of millions of dollars related to actual and potential company losses each year. Aaron, the vice president of the company, once told her, "Peggy, you have personally saved us more than a billion dollars."

Peggy called him as soon as the bar-code man left.

"Aaron," she said, "what's going on? Some man I never met just went through everything on this floor except my personal belongings and cataloged it without explanation. Is there a theft problem in my department?"

"Not as far as I know," Aaron said. "We hired a consultant who told us that theft prevention can be a huge revenue savings in a company our size."

"Even when there isn't a theft problem?" Peggy asked.

Aaron dodged the question. "We hired the consultant to find these issues," he said. "The decision has been made; it's out of my hands."

For her entire career, Peggy had felt trusted. Trust had been conveyed consistently by expecting people to behave appropriately and allowing them the autonomy to conduct their jobs at their discretion. There were guidelines, of course, but people at all levels of the organization were given a wide berth to make decisions. When mistakes were made, they were reviewed, but without punishment or consequence unless there was a moral failing or a consistent deficit.

Without warning or explanation, the company communicated that the most basic level of trust—not to steal the company's property—was broken. Peggy and others felt accused without reason.

The company seemed to have created an arbitrary new rule. The rule was at the expense of destroying their relationship with committed employees. People began to wonder who must be stealing that prompted this micromanaged effort to keep people from taking the company's lamps home.

Our minds tend to ponder many things after an uncomfortable event, both consciously and unconsciously. In this case, Peggy's feelings continued to bother her. In an instant, a company she had served for her entire adult life had suggested that they did not trust her, her supervisors, her colleagues, or her friends, and the impact was significant.

If the company did not trust its employees with something as basic as not stealing a desk lamp, then how could those same employees think that the company would trust their professional judgment and opinions with millions of dollars at stake? If they were to be nothing but potted plants in a management flowchart, why should they stay late, work harder, collaborate closely, or trust anyone else, or trust the company as a whole? Discretionary decisions no longer felt safe, as Peggy and others did their jobs with one eye on the task at hand and the other looking over their shoulders and wondering about job security.

Peggy feared that she had misgauged her employer's commitment and trust. When the company instituted the policy with no transparency or respect shown for the people who had done their jobs long and well, she began to wonder why management had implemented a strategy to fix a problem that didn't exist. This led her to question other decisions the company made. When her boss told her not to worry about a new personnel policy or questioned a hiring decision, she had little faith in the company's motives. She no longer felt safe to try new strategies or to honestly share concerns with her boss or colleagues. The mistrust led her to be more closed off, to protect herself from making mistakes rather than exploring possibilities.

Peggy recognized that her feelings were hurt. She began to re-sent her bosses. Once she felt her own trust had been violated, she was unwilling to trust others or to be vulnerable. It made her unable to honestly engage with those she supervised. Mistrust runs both uphill and downhill. She no longer looked for opportunities to innovate and improve; instead she guarded against mistakes and blame. It was not fight or flight. Instead, it was freeze and hope not to be caught in the crosshairs of something she could not predict. An untrusting and unpredictable environment raises stress, reduces productivity, and erodes personal relationships and job satisfaction.

Had Aaron come to Peggy to address the new policy and honestly share his own feelings about it, she might have felt safer. He could have chosen to share things with Peggy that might have made him subject to criticism from his own bosses. A candid conversation would have been a show of trust toward Peggy's ability to hold potentially damaging information in confidence. People can still work well in an organization that makes decisions they don't like. Trust is not always that the best result will happen, but that the people who will be affected will be encouraged and treated with respect in an effort to achieve the best result. But if the conflict between unpopular decisions transforms into a conflict between the fundamental trust colleagues have in one another, it is very difficult for that organization to have a long and healthy relationship with the workers who keep it alive.

The Trust Equation

Business professor David Maister suggests that some behaviors foster trust and other behaviors erode it. He offers four characteristics that affect whether trust grows or diminishes:

» *Credibility (words).* I can trust what he says about…

» *Reliability (actions).* I can trust her to…

» *Intimacy (emotional safety).* I can be vulnerable with low risk of harm… (While they are not interchangeable, I often use *transparency* and *vulnerability* instead of *intimacy*.)

» *Self-orientation (motives).* I can trust that he cares about more than himself…

Using these four qualities, Maister and his colleagues created the "trust equation."[1] For the purposes of my own analysis of trust and its role in conflict engagement, I have replaced "intimacy" with "vulnerability," which I will explain as we work through the equation. I also use "self-orientation" interchangeably with "self-interest."

$$\text{TRUST} = \frac{\text{CREDIBILITY} + \text{RELIABILITY} + \text{VULNERABILITY}}{\text{SELF-ORIENTATION}}$$

When we are talking to an accountant who has her college diploma and CPA certification hanging on the wall, we will likely trust what she says about accounting—she is *credible.* If we hear from others that she has completed their taxes on time, then we will trust her to complete ours in a timely manner—she is *reliable.* These are the characteristics of trust that are generally the easiest to identify and quantify. They are kind of "pay to play" indicators. Without them, trust is harder to earn, although we might still choose to trust for our own personal reasons.

It is the last two characteristics—vulnerability and self-interest—that catapult people into a higher level of being trusted. As vulnerability increases, trust increases. As self-interest decreases, trust increases. The more guarded I am, the less someone is likely to trust me. The more I focus on myself, the less someone is likely to trust me.

---

1   David H. Maister, Charles H. Green, and Robert M. Galford, *The Trusted Advisor* (New York: The Free Press, 2000), 69–70.

Let's take the example of the accountant. We already know she is credible and reliable because she's responsive, she's experienced, and she has the right letters by her name.

"I've finished your tax return," Stephanie tells me, "but there are some issues I want to discuss."

"That doesn't sound good," I respond, with a rising knot in my stomach.

"It's nothing to worry about, but I want you to know that we cannot always predict how the IRS will treat certain deductions," she says.

"You've spent a substantial amount of your teaching income on books and meals for your students," she continues. "While that is a legitimate expense, because it's disproportionate, they could question it and take away the deduction. I've included it for you, but I can't promise you how it will be treated, and you could face additional tax and some penalty."

Stephanie is admitting that the deduction is a risk, and she wants me to know. She is also admitting that she does not know everything. She is making herself vulnerable by confessing that she does not know everything and suggesting a course of action, even though there is no guaranteed outcome with the IRS.

"If the IRS questions this deduction," she promises, "I'll represent you for free on any appeal."

Now Stephanie has also communicated that she is more committed to her relationship with her client than she is to making every dollar she can. She is confident in her suggestion and is less self-oriented than we might expect. She is willing to go to bat for me if she is mistaken.

None of us is without self-interest. Our point of view exists within us, and we see the world through our unique lens. However, we all have the ability to reach beyond our self-orientation. Keep in mind, though, that altruism can be very self-serving. Giving to others, as helpful as it may be, also boosts our self-interest and perhaps our self-esteem. This does not mean we shouldn't give, but it does mean that we need to be aware of our motives and our desires to the extent possible. My personal observation has been that those who are generous without requiring payback are able to wear life a little more lightly than those who scramble to get what they "deserve."

To Trust or Not to Trust? You Decide.

Solving the trust equation comes easily at first. After all, credibility and reliability are a baseline for most people to achieve a modicum of success as worker, family member, or friend. It is increased vulnerability combined with decreased self-interest that distinguishes those who rise to the highest level of trust.

Earlier I talked about my flight from law school. Len Fromm, the dean of students, withdrew me from classes, gave me a one-year leave of absence, and wrote me a personal note saying "the unexamined life is not worth living." I had earned none of his kindness.

Certainly he earned a salary for doing his job, but he did much more. He worked seventy-hour weeks, caring for students' needs. He learned the names of all two hundred incoming students and matched them to their pictures so he could call new students by name before they even knew who he was. When students came to him with problems, he would sometimes share parts of his own difficult story that did not always show him in the most positive light.

His vulnerability and his focus away from selfishness led to literally thousands of students trusting his goodwill toward them without question. It did not mean that every suggestion Dean Fromm made resulted in the desired outcome, but the level of personal trust is not dependent on outcome; it's based in the relationship.

Why are vulnerability and reduced self-interest so difficult to internalize? Some of it is human nature. It takes confidence and personal security to risk vulnerability because there are those who will exploit it, though not most. More often people who have been given information that makes us vulnerable will respond as if they have become caretakers of something sacred. That kind of trust promotes reciprocity and intimacy.

I can choose vulnerability or others can discover vulnerability in me. Intimacy, on the other hand, is that special relationship that can happen when two or more people become mutually vulnerable.

At first, this may seem to counter my belief that we choose to give trust as much as we demand that people earn it, but I think on deeper exploration it supports the argument. Each of the characteristics of trustworthiness is born out of personal choice. We can choose to get the experience, education, or training that makes us credible to others. We can choose to repeatedly engage in behavior that shows that our word is good, confirming reliability. We can choose to ask for help or to honestly reveal parts of ourselves displaying vulnerability.

The behaviors that support these three qualities create connections that go beyond caring for others and allow them to also care for us. As we become more credible, reliable, and vulnerable, people will be more willing to trust us. For those who are mathematically inclined, these are the numerators of the equation. The bigger these numbers are, the more trustworthy we become.

The final factor, the denominator, is self-orientation. The simple summary is this: The less selfish I am, the more people trust me. The more selfish I am, the less people trust me. And really, doesn't this make sense?

There is a curious irony once again that as we risk being hurt and think of others before ourselves, we are likely to be more trusted and more meaningfully connected with others. This will not eliminate conflict, but trust offers a space that does not require perfection. It does not mean that our vulnerability or trust won't be violated. But if we are not willing to risk intimacy or vulnerability, we are left in a closed world that is only about us. On our own, most of us are pretty small packages indeed.

In conflict, vulnerability and "other-focus" can involve incrementally trusting someone who may have violated our trust. This involves abandoning resentments and offering forgiveness. It can be too dangerous and a bad choice in some circumstances, but it may be one worth considering. After all, when we violate another's trust in us, don't we want another chance—an opportunity to be redeemed? We cannot control how others respond to forgiveness and trust, but we can choose to offer it as a thoughtful risk, not as a blind investment.

I have two examples with different outcomes. In one, I had made a mistake and sent the other lawyer a letter of apology about some documents we had missed and failed to produce to him and his client. I asked him how he wanted to deal with it. He answered me by filing a motion with the court, attached my letter of apology as an exhibit to the motion, and asked the court to sanction me. Although I was angry and felt like he violated my trust when I had admitted my mistake, I still felt better about my actions. I screwed up and could not control his response.

In another circumstance, I made a mistake in how a mediation was handled. The case settled anyway, but in spite of me, not because of me. I called the lawyers to apologize and refunded my fee. Both lawyers have continued to work with me, with a full understanding that I sometimes fall short of the mark.

When it comes to trust, as with most aspects of life, our control is limited. We can choose whether we trust or forgive others, but not how they respond. We can control our own behavior to make ourselves more trustworthy, but we cannot control whether others will, in fact, trust us. We can only create an environment or behave in a way that increases those chances. We cannot demand trust; we can only invite it. To be trusted is not an entitlement; it is a gift from someone else.

In every conflict, nearly without exception, one side or the other will need to make a decision to be vulnerable and other-focused.

Once one person chooses to be vulnerable to someone else, the other person has one of three choices:

1. To care for that vulnerability and reciprocate

2. To exploit that vulnerability to their own advantage

3. To remain warily neutral

You will learn much about yourself and others through the choices you make to risk vulnerability and by how you respond when someone makes themselves vulnerable to you. My own experience is that thoughtful steps into vulnerability promote not only more trust but more happiness.

Going back to the example of Peggy and her boss, we can see that the trust between them was damaged. They had previously shared a long-term professional relationship in which credibility and reliability had never been questioned. Bar-coding all the business's property sent a message of mistrust from the company. Aaron chalked it up to corporate policy without further explanation, leaving Peggy feeling hurt and dismissed. Peggy might have chosen to be transparent about her hurt feelings and anger at being mistrusted. Instead, she elected to pull back and be less vulnerable and focus on her self-interest to avoid having her fears recognized. Aaron failed to notice that Peggy felt her trust had been violated and that she was hurt. Without casting blame on either Peggy or Aaron, what is clear is that as they were more protective and less vulnerable, trust, the relationship, and maybe even happiness became the victims.

Of course, even if they had risked being vulnerable, generous, or forgiving, it's still possible that one or both of them could have been hurt. Most certainly they would have felt fear, discomfort, and uncertainty. But whether they would have worked through that toward a better end, we'll never know.

Harry's Mistake

When I make a mistake that damages someone's trust in me, I want quick forgiveness and a return to the status quo. I want mercy. If someone wrongs me in a way that damages my trust in them, my first inclination is to demand a price for them to "earn" my forgiveness. I want justice according to my definition of it. But for trust to work it can't assume perfection. The best people make mistakes, and the worst people do some good things. As I have said before, we are better than the worst things we do and not as good as the best things we do. Trust leaves room for forgiveness and mistakes.

Harry was a CPA who had helped a now enormous family business from its inception. Whenever anyone called or contacted Harry, he promptly returned calls, emails, and texts. This was true whether it was the founders, the managers, or a frontline employee.

During some complicated tax planning, as the business prepared to transition to the second generation of family members, Harry failed to make an election with the IRS. Before anyone else found out what had happened, Harry went to the owners, Andy and Evelyn, and told them of the mistake and possible consequences.

"This is not a conversation I want to have," Harry began. "I failed to make an election that any novice CPA should have caught. It may not be fixable and could cost millions of dollars. I have no excuse. I have put my malpractice carrier on notice. You need to consult with your lawyers about how to proceed."

Harry followed the meeting with a letter to the owners, confirming what had happened. He sent a copy to his malpractice insurer.

"Thanks for telling us," Andy and Evelyn said almost at the same time. "We'll talk it over and give you a call. I can't tell you how much we appreciate your honesty."

Harry left, and Andy and Evelyn set up a meeting with their children, who would be taking over the business.

"Harry made an accounting error that could cost a few million dollars," Andy and Evelyn told Charles and Maureen. "He's put his malpractice carrier on notice and suggested that we talk with our lawyer and another accountant."

"What do we need to do to make the claim?" Charles and Maureen asked.

"We're not going to make a claim," Andy and Evelyn said.

"You've got to be kidding us," Charles said in disbelief. "This isn't personal against Harry, and besides, his malpractice carrier will pay it."

Maureen nodded her agreement.

"Harry was with us when we started this business in the garage of our little house," Evelyn said firmly but with understanding for her children's frustration. "He worked with us even when we couldn't afford to pay him. We are going to be transferring a business worth hundreds of millions of dollars to the two of you. We have no intention of making a claim against Harry, but we understand that you may want to talk with your own lawyers."

Harry's conduct in the wake of the error confirmed the value and trust Andy and Evelyn had always placed in the relationship. It was not something that could be measured in dollars.

So, where did the conflict exist in this scenario? There was no conflict for Harry. He admitted his error and reported it immediately to his client and his insurance company. Likewise, there was no conflict between Andy and Evelyn and Harry. The trust they chose to place in him was strong enough to weather a substantial mistake. The value in the relationship transcended the money. Andy and Evelyn were not interested in a malpractice case, no matter how financially damaging the tax mistake.

There was no moral failing on the part of Charles and Maureen. They had simply done a cost/benefit analysis and determined that the outcome of bringing a claim outweighed any damage to the relationship. From their perspective, Harry's mistake amounted to a violation of their trust, and his admission confirmed it. Charles and Maureen saw this as a transaction. Andy and Evelyn valued it as a relationship. They did not want an insurance claim to be the coda to their relationship. They knew that their children would not keep Harry as the accountant for the company, but they were not going to end the relationship with a lawsuit.

Over the years, Harry had become a friend and intimate advisor to Andy and Evelyn. He had offered them wise counsel during turbulent family times that had nothing to do with taxes. However, he'd had little involvement with Charles and Maureen.

When the mistake was made, Harry anticipated the consequences and chose to own his role. He didn't try to fix it, hide it, or minimize the potential loss. Though his reliability and credibility were shaken, his vulnerability and lack of selfishness magnified the trust with Andy and Evelyn.

Charles and Maureen hired a lawyer who advised them that they had a valid claim that was likely worth several million dollars.

Andy and Evelyn asked Harry to hire another accounting firm that he thought best to attempt to fix the mistake, and they never made a claim against him. They would have been within their rights to insist he front the bill for the lawyers and accountants who worked to correct the error, but they didn't. The cost of the error was reduced but not eliminated.

Charles and Maureen would have made a different decision to pursue the claim, and there would have been nothing wrong with that decision. They had a different relationship and a different level of trust.

Trust does not come without costs; we just don't know in advance what the costs will be. Here there was a balancing of relationship and money, and Andy and Evelyn placed a higher value on the relationship than in recouping the financial loss. That is not to say the relationship did not have a cost. If the mistake could have bankrupted the company, perhaps they would have considered differently.

Certainly not every mistake has quite such a happy ending—at least from the perspective of those who are affected by it. Even in this example, the retelling of the story would not be the same for the two different generations involved. The senior generation saw this as a triumph of relationship over money. The younger generation saw this as a mistake paid for by the wrong party.

The Absence of Mistrust

Perhaps the best way to embody the trust equation is simply by being kind. When I am kind to someone else, I let them have the biggest piece of pie or even the last piece, literally and metaphorically. It is expressing kindness, generosity, and forgiveness to others—even those outside of my family or group, and perhaps even those who don't deserve it at all. This is what we might call *grace*, or what some describe as *unmerited favor*. Offering grace comes with no expectation of a return. With grace, there is no quid pro quo. There is freedom in less selfishness, because I have already decided that what I have is just fine without any need to compare it with what someone else has. Generosity and grace that promote trust have nothing to do with financial wealth.

Among the best displays of this in my own law practice were two clients, Fred and Georgia. Fred and Georgia were a married couple in their fifties who lived in a small apartment. Fred repaired small engines for a living, and Georgia bagged groceries at a local supermarket.

We represented them in a personal injury case, and Fred and Georgia recovered an amount of money almost equal to the total of their annual income. They came in to pick up their check.

"Thank you for allowing us to help you," I began the meeting. "We need to sign some papers, and I have a check for you."

"That is more money than we've ever had," Fred said.

"Sure is," Georgia confirmed.

"What are we going to do with it?" Fred asked.

"Don't know," Georgia responded. "We already have all we need."

"Guess we better find someone who needs it and let them have it," Fred said.

Georgia nodded in agreement.

And that is just what they did.

This story goes to the heart of internal conflict—that notion that I can only be OK if I have the most, the best, or at least a certain amount of whatever it is. As we talk about later, some of conflict engagement is deciding whether the conflict is worth it. Do I care enough to engage? Already living modestly, when Fred and Georgia had a chance to put a little money aside, they thought they needed to give it to someone who needed it more. Fred and Georgia made a choice to be OK with what they had. They were not weighing the conflict of what they needed to accumulate to be OK in the future. Their actions showed a powerful absence of mistrust in their ability to be OK with where they were.

By the way, being less selfish doesn't mean that I stop wanting things—the better place in line, the next big promotion, or credit for a job well done. It just means I have practiced a bit of humility and have learned that serving myself is an endless task with no satisfactory endgame. An unending quest for self-satisfaction is enormously anxiety provoking. As C. S. Lewis said, a really humble person "will not be thinking about humility; he will not be thinking about himself at all."[2]

Takeaway

We choose both to trust people and expect that they earn it. We can increase the chances that we will be trusted by being more transparent and vulnerable and less self-focused. However, context

---

2   C. S. Lewis, *Mere Christianity*, revised ed. (San Francisco: Harper One, 2015).

matters and the risk may be too costly. Being thoughtful about vulnerability and self-interest is important.

Action

The next time you make a mistake, personally or at work, think about the value of admitting it, without excuse, and offering to make an amend for it in whatever way is most helpful to the other person without focusing on the cost to you. As you think about doing it, notice how energetically you may want to make excuses for the mistake itself or not to make the amend.

9

Engaging with Conflict

Conflict sits on our shoulders, ready for action, from the time we awaken in the morning to the time we go to bed at night. Because conflict is unavoidable, we should be thoughtful about it. By making conscious decisions about our responses to conflict, we can develop confidence, gain wisdom, and improve our relationships. For us to have any chance of being *positively conflicted*, we must do three things:

1. Recognize that the conflict is happening.

2. Decide whether or not to engage in the conflict.

3. When we decide to engage in conflict, do it purposefully.

Without awareness of the conflict and a willingness to own the decision about engaging or not engaging with the conflict, there is little chance, outside of luck, that we can do conflict well. Keep in mind that although we may not be able to accurately point to the cause of the conflict, there is still value in recognizing that we are in conflict.

Recognizing Conflict

Recognizing conflict before it turns into cold-sweat-inducing, full-body-trembling anxiety takes careful intent, focus, and attention. But when we learn to recognize it early, we can limit its more extreme symptoms.

Before the pandemic of 2020 hit the world, I drove three miles to my office to begin my day, and often after that to a different location for the mediation, from Chicago to Cincinnati to Louisville or beyond. Generally, I drove 2,500 miles a month.

Once covid-19 made meeting in person risky, video mediations became the norm. I was not unfamiliar with the technologies for videoconferencing, but I was more often a user than a host. Now I had to learn the applications, deploy them, help others use them, and be ready when anyone among thirty people had an internet failure, a hardware failure, a user failure, or a barking dog, ailing child, frustrated spouse, or aging parent in the background.

This technology learning curve was added to the already challenging job of helping people sort their way through the conflict they had hired me to mediate. My job was no harder than those of the people I saw on my screen who had to address their own conflicts with their lawyers, their bosses, and their families. The technology might be new to them too. Covid, and the different ways people responded to it, became another overlay to an already difficult situation.

Instead of rising early to drive to the office and around the state, I began getting up in the dark and heading down to our basement to do a virtual boxing class and then to read and meditate. I knew I needed to sweat and sit quietly, but neither is my strong suit. Afterward, I'd come upstairs while it was still dark and make my lunch, something I almost never did before. I'd pull multigrain wraps from the fridge and slather on some horseradish hummus. Then I chopped spinach, sliced grape tomatoes along with olives, tossed in some red peppers, and folded them over. Often, I chopped an apple and threw some carrots in a small plastic bag that I used over and over until holes made the bag unusable.

One morning I walked to the office early. The routine was the same. I loaded my black canvas Filson backpack with my laptop and my lunch and plugged my headphones to my phone, considering whether I wanted to listen to a podcast, go with music, or just appreciate the silence of the early morning. Sometimes urban deer would stand within an arm's length of me without running away. A squirrel or a skunk might scurry by. Occasionally I'd pass someone walking their Boston terrier or training for a marathon. The path took me through the foliage of the Indiana University campus and into the town, where people who are homeless might just be getting up to start their days. The scene objectively was passive and relaxed.

When I arrived at my office on this specific morning, I was prepared to do a complicated personal injury case with many lawyers, some of whom I'd worked with before. The plaintiffs and defendants were well represented and nothing was out of the ordinary. By that time, I'd done seventy or so remote mediations.

Then I began to feel sick to my stomach. There was almost a tremor in my hands, and my heart rate rose. My palms began to sweat. I felt a knot in my throat. I went to our breakroom to get a thermometer to take my temperature—normal. My sense of smell was fine. My nose was not runny. I did not have a headache, yet I felt more and more nervous. I called a doctor friend to see what he thought.

"It sounds more like a panic attack than covid," he said. "But if you think you are sick instead of stressed, you should go home."

I didn't think I was sick, but I also didn't think I *should* be stressed. What was there to be stressed about? I called another friend, a counselor.

"You don't sound sick," she said, "but these are strange times. Why don't you try shutting your office door, taking off your mask, loosening your shirt, turning off your lights, and sitting for a few minutes to see if the feelings change."

"That won't help," I said immediately. "I just want some relief."

"Your call," she said. "That's the best I can do."

So I did it. Over fifteen minutes of following my breathing and sitting still in the dark, I stopped sweating, my heart rate calmed, and my head no longer pounded. It was clear that I wasn't sick, but I remained mildly nervous.

Nervousness can be its own conflict. We can call it stress, fear, anxiety, or any one of a number of other words, but it feels like a call to action. It is unpleasant and we want relief. In fact, stress leads us to deny and avoid conflict we might better face.

I was in that place where I did not want to do my job, but I also didn't want to *not* do my job. I had to engage my own conflict before being prepared to engage theirs.

Discomfort was not optional. I could go home and avoid the conflict of the day, which would feel good. Except then I would have to face the conflict of not keeping my commitment to mediate that day.

This vague fear (a hard word to call it) was plaguing me even though I was doing a job I'd done countless times with many of the same people. I don't know if it was pandemic fatigue that seemed to have everyone running on empty or simply my first experience with panic-attack-like symptoms. It turns out that my anxiety was mild and passing, unlike debilitating kinds of panic that some people suffer repeatedly.

All I could process in my mind was that I was uncomfortable. I wondered if I had covid (I was tested and didn't). So I was anxious and afraid for reasons I could not clearly identify—fear of failure, exhaustion, uncertainty generally? I called some people and got outside help because I was unable even to trust myself to make a good decision to stay at work or go home. I got suggestions and followed them. This time they worked, though they might not have. But the outside suggestions were more trustworthy in that moment than my own.

Before I could engage anyone else's conflict, I had to recognize and confront my own. I get hired to help other people with conflicts. I thought I shouldn't struggle with my own—as if I were the exception. I'm not. Sometimes with conflict and fear, our intellectual abilities and past practices are insufficient. Our thinking narrows and tools we might have to help a friend, spouse, or client are nowhere to be found.

I mediated the case, and it resolved, but perhaps because of the skills and insight of the other people involved instead of my own. No one said whether they thought I was different from normal, out of sorts, or muddled, but I felt that way. When the day ended, I was exhausted. Conflict, even when recognized and engaged, tends to wear a person out. I can't tell you that I made the best decision; I just got the bonus outcome.

To Engage or Not to Engage: a Personal Process

We have touched briefly on Kübler-Ross's stages of grief—denial, anger, bargaining, depression, and acceptance. When conflict is first recognized, the first three come into play. Denial kicks in when one or both people think, "Surely this is not a conflict. I'm so clearly right." The next step is anger, when they both think, "How can they be challenging whether I'm right about this?" There may be a partial transition to bargaining as each thinks, "I'll just explain it a little differently or with a different tone, and then they'll see they are wrong." When that doesn't work, denial and anger can quickly return. It is not linear, and the progression can fold back in on itself.

As the struggle between denial, anger, and bargaining continues, if one or both parties realize that all they have done is recognize a conflict, then other choices present themselves. This is scary as the parties realize that neither of them is changing. There is a decision to be made—to engage or not. Unless they have some practice with effective tools, this realization feels hopeless and depressing. Denial has left the building. Avoidance instead of engagement calls loudly. Avoiding and engaging remain as equally available options but ones to more thoughtfully consider. It is a time to weigh options rather than just instinctively react.

BATCE

A tool to have available when considering whether to step into or away from conflict is a concept I call BATCE—best alternative to conflict engagement. BATCE is not unlike BATNA—best alternative to a negotiated agreement. BATNA is a common term used when teaching negotiation. When people are in a negotiation, say, to buy a car, part of the calculus of the process is to weigh the alternative to not negotiating or reaching an agreement. The alternative in this case might be not to buy a car at all, to consider different cars, or to consider a different place to buy a car. There are multiple factors such as price, urgency of need, and the time and uncertainty of looking other places.

BATCE is similar. It is like the self-help resource of conflict choices. In those cases in which engaging the other person in a conflict presents risks we don't wish to take, we still need ways of positively engaging with the discomfort the conflict creates. BATCE helps us come up with those ways.

An Unfair Warehouse

Carlos worked in a fulfillment warehouse for an international e-commerce retailer. The work was physical and the hours were long—routinely ten to twelve hours for five or more days a week. Carlos was from Mexico and was married to an American woman. They had two children. Their youngest was four weeks old, and Carlos's wife, Lexi, was on maternity leave from work without pay. Carlos had a green card. Their family lived paycheck to paycheck, and Carlos's income was essential to keeping their family afloat. To help make ends meet, he worked side jobs installing tile.

The supervisors at the company Carlos worked for were judged on how much product was moved, and that depended on how quickly the frontline workers got trucks unloaded and product moved. The workers got two short breaks during their shifts. Carlos was struggling with the attitude and behavior of his supervisor, Gus.

"Hey, boss, can I get some help unloading this truck?" Carlos asked Gus.

"Come on, Carlos," Gus responded, "you can unload a truck faster than any two people working here."

"That's the point," Carlos said. "I'm getting punished for doing good work. You're not asking anyone else to unload a truck by himself."

"You Mexicans are just harder workers," Gus said. "Something about that southern sun makes you tough."

"That's just not right. If I have to keep lifting hundred-pound boxes by myself, I won't be working at all."

"Not my problem. We have a whole stash of people just waiting for your job. You can't afford to quit, even if you get hurt. I've watched you play with pain."

"What you're doing is completely against the rules," Carlos reminded Gus. "This is all about you hitting your numbers."

"What if it is? Go to HR if you want to, muchacho," Gus replied.

Carlos returned to unloading another truck. When his shift ended, he went home exhausted to Lexi and their children.

"They have no right to treat you that way," Lexi said.

She was also exhausted from taking care of two children and worrying about money.

"Maybe you should go to HR. What Gus is doing can't be OK," Lexi said as she chased their toddler and tried to clean off the kitchen table.

"You aren't brown with a green card. Technically I have rights, but they can make my job even worse, and Gus knows it."

"What alternatives do you have?"

"Maybe none. I've seen what happens to people who rock the boat. It isn't pretty."

Lexi called a friend who knew a lawyer. After hearing Carlos tell the story, the lawyer, Nettie, laid out some options.

"There's nothing OK about how your boss is making you work or the racial references he is making. We could bring a claim with the Equal Employment Opportunity Commission. But it'll take time, and you're basically a gnat on an elephant in terms of leverage. You'll also need coworkers to be witnesses to what's going on, and some people won't talk under oath the same way they talk privately."

"No one will want to risk their own jobs to testify for me. Skip that," Carlos said. "I've seen that play out with coworkers. They give up and move on."

"We could look at a class action. However, you don't get paid any more for being the lead person in a class, and it's a really hard process. There will be lots of appeals."

"No interest there," Carlos said.

"I'm sorry, Carlos," Nettie offered. "The legal options take a lot of time and may make your working conditions worse. I'm willing to do it, but you need to go in with your eyes wide open."

The Best Alternative

Carlos left Nettie's office disappointed, but not hopeless, because he felt like he had some clarity. He saw four options. First, he could continue to engage with Gus. Second, he could go to HR. Third, he could hire a lawyer. Fourth, he could talk to Lexi and come up with a plan to keep the job for now and keep himself as healthy as possible while he worked it.

Carlos and Lexi took a long, hard look at fighting the battle. The practical risks seemed too high, even though Gus's behavior was indefensible. Going to HR would only make Gus mad. Gus had survived there a long time, and Carlos did not think HR was his friend. Lexi was willing to do something legally, but she was not encouraging it. In the end, Carlos and Lexi decided that while it was not fair, they were better off focusing on their BATCE.

They got together with another couple and discussed options. They decided that Carlos would be nice to Gus and do the job (not because Gus deserved it, but because it might make things there better for Carlos). He would take some precautions not to get injured on the job with a back brace and a hand truck to help with lifting. They decided that they could survive doing this for four more weeks until Lexi returned to her job. Meanwhile, Carlos could look for something else or see if he could expand his tile business.

There is nothing fair about this. Gus's behavior was wrong. Carlos would have been fully justified in going to HR or hiring a lawyer. However, Carlos and Lexi did not feel like their circumstances made those their best choices, no matter how right they were. It was a difficult decision not to engage, but they decided it was their best option for now.

Everyone gets to make their own choices, but their life experiences and circumstances influence those choices. Carlos was an immigrant. Even though he was legally in the United States, he did not feel fully supported by the system. As a frontline hourly employee at a big company, he had rights, but he had seen people in his circumstances suffer for exercising those rights. There may have been a legal remedy, but it had its own risks.

Sometimes the most important part of conflict engagement is to decide whether the risks and rewards make it worth it. Carlos and Lexi decided it wasn't, but only after considering their options. Their hope was to use their BATCE to help them endure the conflict while they explored ways to change their circumstances.

Considering BATCE—the alternatives to engagement—is vitally important in deciding whether to engage or not. There are no gold stars for engagement. Pain-free options are few and far between. It is important to respect people's decisions not to engage, if that is what they believe is best for them.

Engagement

It is not easy to decide to engage in conflict, considering the fact that all conflict creates discomfort, and it is our natural inclination to avoid discomfort. As we saw in Carlos's story, there may be times when a person decides that engaging in a conflict is a bad or dangerous choice. In some cases, what feels like avoidance is actually a self-preservation tactic our brains and bodies enact to keep us safe. If your gut is telling you to retreat, don't ignore it. Your gut should be part of the decision-making loop. But it should not be the exclusive arbiter of whether you engage in conflict, as some gut rumbling is part of even minor conflicts.

If you feel uncomfortable but not unsafe, then engagement may be a good choice. Once you have gone through the process of recognizing the existence of conflict, paused to consider your alternatives, and decided to engage, then it is time for you to take positive steps to move through the conflict.

Carlos's use of BATCE showed that social and economic power strongly influence our decision to engage or not to engage in conflict. If we have enough social and economic power, engaging in conflict is an option that's easier to choose.

Irene was a sales and delivery driver for a large beverage company. She was the only woman on her team. She made a decision a long time ago to deflect rather than engage the disrespectful and insulting comments from some of her male team members. However, when those insults became more persistent and she began to feel unsafe, she considered alternatives.

Irene's husband, Steve, was a construction foreman. He presided over large construction projects and had a very stable income. He'd long encouraged Irene to complain to management or quit.

For Irene and Steve, the BATCE of continuing to tolerate the behavior and look for ways to endure it was not appealing. They had enough money from Steve's income, and Irene's position in the larger community was secure. Irene did not have to continue to live with the bad behavior.

Irene went to HR and complained, knowing that even if they made her life difficult, she and Steve had enough money to survive until she found something else.

When HR did not come through for her, Irene began documenting and recording what was happening and went to a lawyer, who filed a claim with the EEOC.

Irene was being treated badly, but she had the economic safety net that allowed her to decide to engage. The alternative to engaging in the conflict—putting up with a hostile work environment—was not worth it...largely because her family was not economically threatened by her decision to engage. She also did not have the underlying tension of worrying about a green card.

Irene and Carlos each worked in bad work environments. Their decisions to engage or not were driven by their personal evaluations of their alternatives to engagement, not only by whether they were right. They were both right, but one had economic and personal security that made engagement less threatening. There is no element of fairness in the assessment. Each made a decision that they thought was best for their unique circumstances.

Do Conflict Better

Our feelings often dictate our behavior. So if a conflict makes us angry, we frequently lash out at the other person. If we are unwilling to break this cycle, we ensure that conflict will worsen and repeat itself. That is why I generally use the phrase "do conflict better." The practice is not to *feel* better, although that may be a by-product of *doing* better. Thinking better might help you to do better. But if we wait to think or feel better before we take action, we might never do better. Only when we choose to behave differently from how we feel (and sometimes how we think) in the midst of disagreement do we have the potential to influence our impact on the conflict.

As we practice behaving differently in response to conflict, we might see our feelings evolve as a result of the behavior. Choosing our behavior requires self-awareness, as opposed to self-absorption. It also requires us to pay close attention to what others say and do. And sometimes it takes suggestions from others for us to see and choose options that at first blush don't appeal to our way of thinking.

When feeling hopelessly snared in a conflict, these outside ideas can break a logjam of righteous thinking that leaves us unable to decide or act at all. Lloyd is a childhood friend, and we talk regularly. He knows that I sometimes get paralyzed trying to make just the right decision. My natural approach leaves me making no decision at all. After hearing me endlessly wrestle with one decision, Lloyd suggested, "You don't think your way to right action. Sometimes you have to act your way to right thinking."

If this seems backward, do your own test at work or home. When you are struggling and someone makes a proposal that you've never considered, is your first instinct to tell them why it won't work? What would happen if you took the suggestion and accepted the outcome?

Having spent years struggling with his own approach to life, my friend Dewey started taking suggestions, even though they sometimes made no sense to him. His life improved, but he was still puzzled. "I know this works in practice," Dewey said, "but does it work in theory?"

Could the change in behavior have value if the theory was beyond Dewey's understanding? Have you ever wanted to discount something positive because you did not understand it? Though it feels counterintuitive to behave in a way we do not feel, there are times when it becomes a necessary factor in breaking the cycle of conflict and tension. Instead of our circumstances and feelings ruling us, we begin to exert some influence over our circumstances and stop being prisoners of our feelings.

Understanding is a worthy goal, but I sometimes find that I can choose to accept something even when I don't understand it. When I stopped anesthetizing all conflict with vodka, the problems between Patty and me did not magically disappear. My self-focused approach to the world caused many aftershocks that kept us off-balance, and Patty was often waiting for the next disaster to strike. We had to see whether we were both willing to change enough to salvage our marriage.

I had stopped drinking, but I still did not like advice. In spite of years of absence and inattentiveness, I remained overly confident that I had all the answers, if only Patty would listen. Having been on the receiving end of my arrogance, she wasn't too keen to hear.

Unable to resolve things on our own, we went to see a psychologist named Jack. He described a common difficulty for couples struggling after years in the same relationship. "It's like you're trying to dance, but you only know the steps to one tune. No matter what songs are available, you continue to dance with the same steps to the same music. It may not be working but it feels comfortable."

A good therapist or a good friend can help change the tune *and* the dance. Whether we would take Jack's advice and go through the discomfort of stepping on each other's toes to learn a new dance would be up to us. We were undeniably in conflict, with the high stakes of our marriage and family in the balance. We did not have the capacity to change the tune or the dance on our own after we'd spent years hanging on to our way of doing things.

Jack's observation made sense immediately, that is until he asked *me* to change *my* dance steps. He observed that my behaviors, which centered around being physically and emotionally absent, aggravated Patty's concern that I would continue to run away whenever things became difficult. To address Patty's justifiable lack of trust and her hope that I would step into the dance and not run from the ballroom, he made what seemed a very simple suggestion:

"When you come through the door every night, I want you to say, 'I'm home, I'm sober, and I'm glad to be here.'"

Jack's small office got silent.

Consistent with my desire for Patty to change instead of me, I balked at such a simple and silly-sounding sentence. It felt awkward and disingenuous. So I asked him, "What if it's not true? What if I'm home and sober, but *not* glad to be there?"

He paused, then looked at me. "When did telling the truth suddenly become so important to you? Just say it."

This kind of directness might not be in the "how to be a counselor" handbook. It might not be effective with all couples. But it was a very skillful way of confronting me. Did I want our marriage to succeed? Was my way working? Who was I to say what was silly—or perhaps even true?

My behavior and thinking had created a mighty hill that Patty and I would have to climb if we were to overcome our issues and repair our marriage. Besides, what was there to lose by trying the exercise? Though I wasn't yet sufficiently self-aware to accept my role in our struggles, I was just willing enough to see that we had reached the breaking point. Our situation had become desperate, and if I wasn't open to surrendering to something beyond my own failed thinking, there would be no saving us. The pride that guarded my fear of change yielded to my fear of losing our marriage. For many months after this session, when I walked in the door each night, I announced, "I'm home, I'm sober, and I'm glad to be here."

It was awkward. It was embarrassing. And sometimes it was flat-out dishonest. But was it really dishonest? If we take the long view, I was doing exactly what I was "glad" to do. I wanted to be married. I may have occasionally walked in the door when I was not glad to be there at that moment, but for grown-ups there are more important things than ephemeral feelings. No matter how compelling a feeling is in the moment, it will not likely remain constant unless we nurture it to do so. Motivations for our behaviors are multidimensional. It is helpful to get perspectives and suggestions from others, and to take a long view rather than a short one.

I am certainly glad to have said it and glad still to be there.

What I've learned through my relationships and through my career as a mediator is that there are times when our feelings lag behind our behavior, so feelings might not be the best motivator or the best divining rod of what we want in the big picture. Often, we get so invested in our own emotions in the moment that we decide we can only change our behavior after we understand it or feel a certain way about it.

Sometimes behavior needs to precede understanding. This is not only true in marriages, but in businesses, friendships, families, and the world at large. A valuable lesson I learned was that when my way is not working, there is often no harm following a trusted person's suggestion that makes no sense to me. After all, *my* sensible approach has been getting me precisely to a place I do not want to be.

Though it feels counterintuitive to behave in a way we do not feel, there are times when it becomes a necessary factor in breaking the cycle of conflict and tension. Instead of our circumstances ruling us, we begin to exert some influence over our circumstances by doing something different. It frequently happens when we do something that we don't want to do or that does not feel "fair." From that very behavior, we can imagine things that were previously unimaginable.

Many years later, Patty and I were visiting friends. I was sitting in the corner of the room, mostly reading, when I overheard bits of a conversation between Patty and her friend Laura. Patty was describing this time in our marriage, which Laura had observed firsthand.

"Every night, without exception, Sam walked in the door and said, 'I'm home, I'm sober, and I'm glad to be here,'" Patty told Laura.

"You know," Patty said, casting a brief glance in my direction, "it seems like such a small thing, but the fact that he was willing to do it, and that he eventually came to mean it, was so important."

"Did you ever tell him that?" Laura asked.

"No," Patty said, looking across the room to make sure I heard, but saying nothing more.

What had seemed silly and inconsequential to me at the time was enormously important to healing a relationship in peril. We were both struggling to see past the conflict and rebuild the trust that had so seriously deteriorated. Our conversations had become nothing but sad points and counterpoints. We needed different tunes and different dance steps, and they were all uncomfortable. After years of blaming circumstances or each other, we worked to change ourselves and to accept each other. It was not always pretty, but it was consistent, committed, and unthwarted by circumstance or discomfort. Our marriage has endured for decades beyond this very painful time, but I'm not sure it would have without both of us making changes that didn't always initially resonate. It is in our most intimate relationships that we get to practice how we deal with conflict, and then we have a chance to take the lessons we learn into the wider world of the conflicts we face in all our interactions.

Here I want to emphasize that I can only talk about *my* discomfort and efforts to change. Patty made her own decision to work through trust and change issues, and I would not claim to know what all of them were, fully understand them, or grasp how hard they were. In the throes of serious conflict, everyone experiences pain and makes hard choices. In considering our own efforts to change, we may overestimate our impact and fail to perceive and appreciate the massive and sometimes sacrificial efforts of others. Compassion for the struggles of others, even those we find most irritating, is an often absent but vital skill in navigating conflict.

Behaving differently from how we feel is an essential part of improving our relationship with conflict. Although these lessons originally grew out of alcoholic behavior and a struggling marriage, what I learned transcended addiction. Listening to others and being open to the possibility that I could be wrong changed my life.

Takeaway

To engage in conflict requires both awareness and choice. Whether we do it requires us to face the reality that all conflict involves pain now or pain later. Sometimes decisions about whether or not to engage can be driven by uniquely unfair circumstances.

Action

The next time you feel the physical effects of conflict with someone at work or at home, take a moment to see if they seem to be experiencing the circumstance the same way you are. Decide if the conflict is important enough for you to take the risk of telling them that your feelings are hurt and why. While that kind of vulnerability would not have helped Carlos or Irene, considering it as an option, even if you reject it, can inform a decision. It may or may not be worth the risk, but the exercise of looking beyond yourself and owning the decision can be very helpful in taking control where you can and not being overly distracted by resentment.

10

Embracing the Discomfort

I address conflict for a living. My days are spent in mediation, navigating the choppy waters between multiple groups of people in the midst of uncomfortable tension. You'd think by now that jumping into other people's conflicts would be easy. That is not true. When I'm engaged in conflict in a mediation, it is a full-body experience. Practice helps me do it better than I used to, but at some level all conflict is personal, even if you're watching on the sidelines or engaging as an outsider. In fact, part of my job in engaging with others in conflict is to consider my own natural responses so I can have some compassion for and understanding of theirs.

But I don't want to forget how I respond when the conflict is my own. When I find myself in conflict, my physiological response is the same as anyone else's. Say my boss calls me in for a Friday afternoon meeting. I don't know the reason for the meeting, but I've had a disappointing week on the job. Though he's given no indication of looming reprimands or warnings, I feel the tension begin to rise, and before my brain can even process why I feel so nervous, my body is reacting: sweaty palms, rapid heart rate, upset stomach. Will I fight, flee, or freeze? My brain doesn't know, but the rest of me is getting ready.

Were I paying attention to why I was having these symptoms, I might be able to assess the threat level and focus on a plan for productively engaging with my boss. I might consider why I had such a poor week and what solutions I might give to assure my supervisor it won't happen again. Instead, I'm focused solely on my physical and emotional reaction to the potential conflict, and there's little attention left to analyze the situation rationally. My mind and body are wrapped up in the discomfort of my own fear of the unknown as I imagine the worst.

For most of us, our dislike of conflict leads to a tendency to deny or avoid the painful reality of difficult circumstances. We *can* choose to engage with conflict differently, though. To do so requires that we embrace the fact that discomfort is inevitable, recognize the ways we attempt to avoid the discomfort so that we can mitigate them, take a moment to reflect on the situation, and perhaps even look for ways to not take ourselves so seriously as we move through the conflict. Before we can do any of those things, however, we must choose to pay attention.

Pay Attention

French philosopher Simone Weil once said, "Attention is the rarest and purest form of generosity."[1] Ms. Weil died in 1943, well before the introduction of attention suckers like TVs, smartphones, and tablets. Imagine, then—if attention was considered a rare form of generosity in the first half of the last century, how much more precious must it be now?

---

1   Simone Weil, *First and Last Notebooks: Supernatural Knowledge* (Oxford University Press, 1970).

Attention is certainly a gift, but it is one we bestow somewhat recklessly. Though we find it easier to pay attention to ourselves, even this can be scattered and inconsistent, depending on the various stimuli that assault us on a daily basis. It's easy to miss internal signs, namely discomfort, that alert us to being in conflict.

Every time we experience discomfort, we are also experiencing conflict. Some discomfort is so minor we hardly notice it, or we fix it immediately, but this does not negate the fact that for those seconds or minutes, we were in conflict with something or someone, including ourselves. By learning to acknowledge these microdiscomforts and their accompanying conflicts, we can practice recognizing bigger, more important conflicts. Recognizing the discomfort—paying attention to it—is the first step in meaningful conflict management. Awareness also helps us to avoid engaging in denial and to become more accepting of our circumstances while honing techniques to work through them. And awareness of our own discomfort allows us to read other people better.

As we have discussed, fear is nearly always at the heart of conflict. To better recognize the symptoms that signal fear and conflict, it's important that we pay attention to both our physical and emotional cues. Physical or emotional discomfort is a sign that something is other than the way we wish it to be. More often than not, there is an underlying fear of losing something we have or of not getting something we want.

Physical responses to fear include a knotted stomach, clenched teeth, and tight shoulders. Emotional responses might include sadness, anger, frustration, or embarrassment. Many of us are more attuned to either the physical symptoms of fear or the emotional ones.

Because fear exists on a spectrum, it can be difficult to identify that we're feeling it when it's at the lower end, particularly when it involves something we may not consider worthy of our concern. Fear can be as subtle as a vague but unsettling feeling of anxiety when going to work at the same job we went to yesterday, when nothing seems to have changed, and where yesterday we felt just fine.

Paying attention to our feelings is critical for engaging with conflict. When we don't stay focused, the natural discomfort resulting from conflict drives our instinctive choices, which may allow us to feel better in the moment while aggravating the tension at the heart of the matter. When Simone Weil identifies the generosity of attention, it should include paying attention to our cues, not living in denial of them.

Pain Versus Pleasure

We are naturally drawn to seek ways to comfort ourselves when we're in the midst of conflict. Our quest for comfort is biological. And it is a tempting little devil. It needn't rely on facts or reason. It just wants comfort for comfort's sake.

As an example, let's say I had a hard day at work and want comfort when I return home. Overeating sweets is a short-term comfort and a long-term plague for me. So, I may choose to sit down and eat an entire package of Oreos. The temporary enjoyment I experience in eating the cookies is swiftly replaced by regret, embarrassment, and—you guessed it—discomfort. The original discomfort I was experiencing led to an entitlement to feel better, and satisfying the entitlement by eating cookies created more discomfort. Sometimes we do this unconsciously.

One night as I was sitting at the kitchen table with a package of Oreos and a quart of milk in front of me, Patty asked, as I reached for another cookie, "Do you even know that you have an Oreo in your mouth?" The embarrassing answer was no. I was not aware enough to enjoy the distraction I had chosen. I was eating cookie after cookie without consciousness. If you had watched my behavior and asked me about it, my embarrassment would reveal my weakness, and I might have lashed out at you. That would not be on you; it would be on me. I was glad Patty pointed it out, but it is always good to consider relationship, context, and importance before calling someone out on their vulnerabilities.

Dr. Drew Westen, a professor at Emory University, document-
ed this phenomenon—the mind's tendency to seek pleasure and
avoid pain—after conducting a remarkable experiment to test this
conclusion.[2] His experiment was not about politics, although the
subjects were sorted by political preference.

At the time, the 2004 presidential election between incumbent
George W. Bush and Democratic challenger John Kerry was heat-
ing up. In the years since 9/11, the two political parties had become
even more fervent in their different beliefs about how the country
should be run. Dr. Westen decided to test how average people responded when confronted with a statement from their candidate
that contradicted what they believed about their candidate.

Two groups of subjects agreed to be placed in an fMRI (func-
tional magnetic resonance imaging) machine, which measures brain
activity in real time. The subjects were divided into Bush supporters and Kerry supporters. Each would enter the machine individually, and based on their political affiliation, Dr. Westen presented
them with factual statements that were in opposition to their political views. The results were astonishing.

The same brain circuits that light up when we experience pain
activated when the subjects were presented with the negative information about their preferred candidate. The stress of the conflict, even just a conflict of ideas, diminished activity in the executive
functioning parts of the brain on which we rely to reason through
problems. Then, with no further stimulus, encouragement, or persuasion, the activity migrated to parts of the brain that respond to
pleasure. Rather than acknowledge facts or evidence that might be
counter to their dearly held beliefs, the brains of the Republicans *and*
the Democrats, without conscious effort, shifted the activity from

---

2   Drew Westen, *The Political Brain: The Role of Emotion in Deciding
the Fate of the Nation* (New York: PublicAffairs, 2007); see also Margaret Heffernan, *Willful Blindness: Why We Ignore the Obvious at Our
Peril* (New York: Bloomsbury, 2011), 44–45.

pain to pleasure. Everyone's brain steered them to ignore conflict and seek pleasure, for no reason other than that it felt better. Pain is uncomfortable, so we retreat, consciously or unconsciously, to pleasure.

We can be so busy seeking relief and comfort that we allow the fear to compromise our thinking. We simply react, often by making suboptimal decisions. A courageous step would be to ask for help, but the vulnerability of admitting the problem fuels the fear. There are psychological reasons beyond the scope of this book, but at its basis, fear stimulates our most primitive responses (eating is one) while diminishing our executive functioning when we most need it. What we really need to do is pause, which is a very unnatural response in the face of significant discomfort.

Press Pause

When I recommend that you *pause* for conflict, what do I mean? Simply, I mean resisting the urge to react. Experience the discomfort that compels you to fight, flee, or freeze by choosing to thoughtfully pause (which is not the same as freezing) instead. Pretend you hold your brain's remote in your hand and hit the pause button to stop the action without losing your place. You can come back here later, but for the moment just stop and reflect. This feels counterintuitive because our biology drives us to seek comfort, and pausing seems to be just about the most helpless thing we can do. Many of us believe we can regain control when it appears we have lost it by doing something, seemingly anything. But when done intentionally, pausing can actually be the most empowering response. As Viktor Frankl says, "Between stimulus and response there is a space. In that space is our power to choose our response. In our response lies our growth and freedom."[3]

---

3   This quote has often been attributed to Viktor Frankl from his book *Man's Search for Meaning*. However, I was unable to find the exact quote in the book.

Still, it's a difficult thing to do. Our physical and emotional reactions to conflict ignite a powerful instinct to react without consideration for the unintended consequences. And the urge to reduce or eliminate pain beckons to us. Rarely are we inclined to extend feelings of discomfort, yet pausing—although it prolongs the discomfort—gives us a moment to gain perspective and consider options. It allows us to consider a more meaningful response. Taking that pause is to admit the reality of the discomfort or pain and accept that we cannot escape it. We can only choose our response.

Some people are naturally reflective, patient, and circumspect when making decisions, regardless of the fear, pain, or conflict they face. I am not one of those people. If there is a conflict or anxiety-provoking issue, I assume there is an action to be taken, and I want to take it. My natural response to discomfort is to do something that moves me back toward comfort, even if it is illusory or possibly damaging. I also might try to fix something that someone does not want fixed. They might be insulted by my inference that something *needs* to be fixed or the insinuation that they couldn't fix it without my unsolicited help. As a dear friend once told me, "The fact that some people seek your advice does not mean all of us want it." Ouch! But so true.

To be clear, I'm not saying that my perception of every conflict is accurate. Nor am I claiming that my rush to action is wise. Quite the opposite. My own lack of wisdom when conflicted illustrates why pausing has value, and if I often mistake it in myself, I had better approach the conflicts of others with a good dose of humility. Unless a real threat to life or limb creates the conflict, pausing is a good choice. It expands the possibilities for analysis, management, and resolution of the conflict.

When I do spend time with people who respond more thoughtfully to conflict than I do, I see a different approach. More thoughtful people consider options, weigh them, and make the best decision possible based on the information they have. They show patience as they process the details of a conflict and resist rushing to wrap things up before giving everything its due consideration. For them, deciding more quickly might create the same discomfort and pain that I feel when pausing. They are more likely to accept that when conflict arises, pain is unavoidable, and therefore, they are more likely to live with the anticipated pain until they can make an informed choice. They also allow others the dignity to struggle through their own conflicts without assuming that they have the answer.

Personally, I'm prone to processing information out loud and thinking that someone will tell me if they feel differently. My approach irritates people who are more circumspect than I am and who process information internally. My tendency is to make a quicker decision that makes me feel better, and then I'm willing to live with the fallout from whatever that decision might be— good or bad. Their tendency is to wait, consider, decide, and then act.[4]

Though it is not my first instinct, this notion of pausing has become an important tool for me. It is not innate, but with practice I have improved. To use it, I have to first recognize discomfort and be willing to live in it for longer than is natural for me. It does not feel good. Sometimes I do well, and sometimes not. If I pay attention to others, I can get a cue about which approach might be most helpful to them.

I should place a disclaimer here that pausing does not promise a perfect response or outcome. Rather, it allows us a moment to reflect and put the discomfort in context. This may help us make a better decision, respond more appropriately, and move through the conflict with greater ease and accept the outcome, whatever it may be, with more equanimity.

---

4   Susan Cain, *Quiet: The Power of Introverts in a World That Can't Stop Talking* (New York: Crown Publishers, 2012).

Amor Towles wrote a novel called *Rules of Civility* about the lives of a group of young people living in New York City. His characters encounter all sorts of emotionally taxing circumstances. One character offers some striking advice for responding to difficult situations: "In moments of high emotion—whether they're triggered by anger or envy, humiliation or resentment—if the next thing you are going to say makes you feel better, then it is probably the wrong thing to say."[5] My paraphrase is "If I'm upset and the retort feels good, don't say it."

If we recognize the physical cues of discomfort and have the discipline and willingness to pause, then we also have the opportunity to choose a response that may be different from the reaction initiated by how we feel. Choice comes with responsibility, but so does reaction.

Pausing Gives Us Time to Make Choices

Once we have recognized conflict and paused to consider our reaction to it, we are then empowered to make a choice about how to respond to it. Having choice and exercising it wisely are two different things, however. To illustrate the impact of choice, I'll relate two incidents from my life in which I found myself in conflict that left me anxious and upset. In one of those incidents, I paused before I made my decision about how to respond. In the other, I made the choice to merely react.

What Don't You Understand?!

When I mediate conflicts, it is not uncommon that the people involved have been negotiating long before the day of mediation. In some cases, they have been going round and round for years before they step into my office. Both parties typically have a strong sense

---

5   Amor Towles, *Rules of Civility* (New York: Penguin Books, 2012).

of where they last left the negotiations, but they do not always have the same recollection.

There are no fixed rules that govern how anyone is required to negotiate when they arrive. Generally, there is an unspoken rule that neither side will go backward from their prior position unless there has been a substantial change that affects the options. It is not so different from buying a car. If the dealer offers to sell you the car for $25,000, you offer him $20,000, and he says, "I've changed my mind, I'm raising my price to $30,000," the conversation usually ends.

The same thing happens in negotiating litigated disputes. The rules aren't written, but they are assumed, and there are consequences for breaking them. If someone has demanded $100,000 to settle a lawsuit and the other side has offered $25,000, then the unspoken rule is that neither of them will make a move that puts them farther apart than when they begin the mediation. The demanding side will not double their demand to $200,000, and the offering side will not reduce their offer by half to $12,500.

However, since that rule is unspoken, it occasionally gets broken. Circumstances sometimes arise when one side or the other *will* go backward. Typically, they will offer a reason as to why they are defying conventional expectations. Then the other side has an opportunity to consider whether the reasons are legitimate or not. When a backward move happens without explanation, people are less willing to continue.

Monica and Brad were experienced legal negotiators representing their clients. They all met first with me in an open discussion about perspectives and process. I then sent each party to their own private room with the attorneys and advisors. From there, the goal was to find any areas of potential agreement—what would nudge them toward resolution.

After private conversations with her clients, Monica lowered her demand from $100,000 to $95,000. I took the offer to Brad's room, we discussed the circumstances, and I asked how he wanted to proceed. Before Brad could speak, his client said, "I'm lowering my offer to $10,000." Brad's client had already offered $25,000 prior to mediating. Now, after the first round of negotiations, we were further apart than where we began.

These folks had hired me to help negotiate and resolve their dispute, and in the first hour I took a $75,000 gap and increased it to $85,000. This is not why people hire mediators and professional negotiators. My pride was tweaked. I was annoyed. As the mediator, I knew how this was *supposed* to work. And Brad's client was interfering with my agenda. Brad stared down at his hands, because he also knew this was not the way it was supposed to work. I could feel the physical effects of my irritation—effects that were likely evident in the tone of my voice when I responded.

My pride was threatened, creating an element of fear. I also felt entitled to a certain treatment from the clients I was trying to help. In the moment, I couldn't separate myself from the conflict enough to realize that disputes belong to the parties involved. They get to do what they want, and what I think about it is ultimately irrelevant. Nevertheless, I pressed on.

"I'm surprised you're going backward," I began, "but are you willing to give me a reason for your change, so I can explain it to the people in the other room?" Brad's client looked at me and said nothing.

Even more annoyed, I detailed what was likely to happen from this sudden impasse. "Monica's client will likely respond in kind," I said. "She'll raise her demand to more than $100,000. Your disagreement will go from $75,000 to $85,000 to more than $100,000, and we'll have accomplished nothing."

Brad's client watched me for an uncomfortably long moment, then put his forearms on the table and leaned toward me. His voice was very low and deliberate when he finally spoke. "Just what part of '$10,000' don't you understand, Sam?"

I was taken aback. "Take the offer to the other room," he ordered, sitting back in his chair and meeting my eyes with a challenging gaze.

I felt my face flush with righteous anger. My process was being hijacked (in my mind), but the key word here was "my." It was not *my* dispute, but *theirs*. I had allowed myself to arrogantly believe that I unilaterally controlled it, and people had to respond as I wished them to—at least as to the process. My job is to pay attention to the people in the rooms and recognize that there is more than one tool—and that I don't control all those tools. My righteousness did no one any good. I'm there to help people have conversations, not judge *how* they wish to have those conversations. Over the years, I have come to believe that people have no obligation to accept my suggestions or proceed according to my agenda. Still, when someone so clearly chooses to ignore both convention *and* me, I don't like it. When the unspoken rules are not followed, I'm as instinctively inclined to call out "no fair" as are the people in the dispute. Instead, I need to practice my own advice and hit pause.

In this case, practice paid dividends. I had learned to recognize the physical and mental discomfort that alerted me to the rising temperature of the conflict. I had also learned to pause in the discomfort. I wanted, in my anger and frustration, to act. But instead I halted to give myself time to reflect. I realized there was nothing I could say to Brad's client that would be helpful. It was his case, and he could use whatever strategy he wished.

There is an embarrassing phrase that describes me well in those entitled moments when I get really irritated with someone else: "A man of my caliber is entitled to…" You can fill in the dots any way you wish.

Please read that with the healthy amount of sarcasm I intend, because I do not consider myself to be a man of any particular caliber, nor do I believe that I'm entitled to any particular response. Having said that, it is clear that I do not always *feel* what my brain already knows. People can treat me however they wish. Their treatment of me is out of my control. All I can do is choose whether or how to respond. Feeling that I am entitled to any particular reaction from someone else sets me up to be resentful and ineffective, and that is profoundly true in conflicts.

Still, *knowing* that I am of no caliber and have no entitlement does not keep me from *feeling* very differently. I cannot separate myself from the human condition of wanting to be valued and treated with respect. Brad's client's response felt insulting to me and to the process, and my raised heart rate confirmed that feeling.

Brad's client, however, seemed perfectly content with his response. As far as I know, he is not a mean-spirited or irrational person. He had a job to do and saw his approach as being reasonable, just as I saw it as irritating and unhelpful. In that moment, we were not likely to agree.

So instead of giving voice to my irritation, I paused and asked if Brad's client minded if we took a break to consider where things stood. It would have done no good for me to explain to Brad's client why his approach would not be effective. At some level, I probably hoped that Brad himself could bail us out from the impasse seemingly caused by his client's approach. Brad's body language suggested that he was about as uncomfortable as I was with his client, but he also respected his client's right to negotiate the case the way he wished. It wasn't Brad's client's first rodeo, and he was well aware that the mediation would probably end. He did not owe me an explanation.

When I returned to the room, I confirmed that Brad wanted me to take the offer as his client presented it. I explained that I thought the process would be over and the other side would leave unless he had some reason to explain why he was going backward.

Brad's client responded, "I don't owe them an explanation, and I don't care if it ends."

I carried the message to the next room without any explanation beyond that I was doing as I was told. Monica gathered up her things and left with her client.

What Brad's client did was out of my control and was certainly not what I wanted to happen. The best I could do was not aggravate the conflict or increase the discomfort by lecturing him or by sitting on my high horse and telling him why I was right and he was wrong. First, I might be wrong, and second, it would not have mattered either way.

In conflicts it is important for me to remember that I never have all the facts and that perceptions of the same set of facts can be very different. Although it may not be at first evident, when two or more sides spend all their time arguing that they are right, it is just a more "civilized" effort to fight power with power. When we are deeply invested in our facts and our perspectives as being uniquely true, we are choosing to prolong conflict. It may feel good in the short run, but it rarely leads to long-term solutions.

Brad and his client left, and the case settled about six months later. I have worked with Brad many times since that day, and I don't know if there was a unique circumstance that dictated his client's approach. By following directions, I respected the decision-maker's control over his own negotiation. He was not interested in my advice, and he didn't have to be. He may have been very well pleased with the outcome. In that moment, the best I could do was not push my agenda any further and not act on my initial physical response. There are no gold stars for not making things worse, but on that day, it was the only benchmark I could achieve. Even this discussion makes it all about me.

The situation with Brad was not the last time I interjected myself righteously into someone else's dispute.

The Loudest Voice

On another occasion, I was in a mediation with a young person who was under the age of eighteen when she was involved in an accident through no fault of her own. Her parents hired attorneys to bring a lawsuit on her behalf since a person cannot make legally binding decisions until they are at least eighteen years old.

By the time of the mediation, several years had passed, and she was now over eighteen and legally in charge of her own case, as well as her own decisions. Although she was old enough to be present without her parents, her mom and dad came to the mediation, along with both of her lawyers from different firms. The woman who was hurt, her parents, and the attorneys were in the same room. In a separate room was another group of people who had been sued and might be held responsible for her injuries.

As the day went on, I went from room to room talking with everyone about the case and the issues that might be presented at trial if we did not settle that day. Parties on all sides were trading settlement proposals and the reasons behind the proposals.

The only people talking in the room with the young woman who had been injured were her parents and one of her lawyers. After several hours, I said to her, "Each time I'm in here, other people describe what happened, how you are, and what you want to happen. I'd like to hear how you feel about it."

Almost before I finished, her lawyer raised his hand, pointed his finger at me, and loudly proclaimed, "Your job is to talk to me. I don't care what she says. I'm her lawyer, and you are to direct all your questions exclusively to me. Do you get that?"

I didn't recognize the heat in my face or the tingling in my hands. I didn't stop to consider my feelings. There was no pause button; or if there was, it was malfunctioning. Instead, I reacted— swiftly, passionately, and with zero consideration for anyone else. I slammed my hand on the table and pointed my finger back at him. "Don't you ever come into my office and tell me you don't care what your client says and tell me not to talk to her!" Then, for good measure, "Do *you* understand?"

Everyone became silent, clearly uneasy with the turn in the tone of the conversation.

I'm not sure exactly how much time passed. It may only have

been a few seconds. It felt like an out-of-body experience. In thousands of mediations, I don't think I've reacted quite like that before or since.

After sitting back in my chair to catch my breath, I slowed down and lowered my voice. "I'm really sorry," I said. "I'm going to go back to my office so you all can chat and decide whether you want me to continue in this mediation or go ahead and fire me now. I apologize to all of you."

When I think back on my behavior, I can manufacture any number of reasons why I responded so inappropriately. None of them excuse it. The reasons I create in my head might be instructive for me to learn a lesson and do my job better, but they are irrelevant to the people involved, and they don't exonerate me. It does not matter whether the other lawyer or I was right about how to communicate and with whom. I exposed a button, and the other lawyer pushed it. I reacted without thinking, and the mediation was heading toward an unresolved end. They could have done better had they never met me.

A half hour passed, and the other lawyer who was in the room representing the young woman knocked on my door. She and I had mediated many cases over the years. She came in, put her hand on my shoulder, and said, "Sam, I knew we had an anger management problem in the other room...I just didn't know it was you." She smiled and patted my arm.

Her response did not excuse my behavior, but it did not further punish me either. Her behavior was also a lesson for me. When someone knows they have behaved badly, telling them again does not help. Rather, pointing it out often promotes defensiveness, minimization, and excuses. Her wisdom was a gift to all of us.

We ended the mediation. I apologized again to everyone, and I did not send a bill. Whatever happened in that case would no longer be influenced by me. My work, poorly executed, was done.

I share this story to illustrate how easy it is for me to encourage people to recognize conflict, pause, and then choose how to respond. As with so much good advice, dispensing it is effortless and following it is hard. Fortunately, this kind of investment in my own emotions is not my normal response, but it is a reminder that regardless of experience and training, we don't always make the best choices. A doctor friend of mine says, "Chemistry beats psychology every time." If he is right, then I need to practice pausing when my chemistry becomes combustible.

The more important the situation and the more pronounced the physical symptoms, the more compelled we feel to react immediately. The more intense the pain, the more intense the desire to alleviate it. Yet it is precisely these situations where pausing and reflecting is so critical.

After thousands of mediations, I recall only one reaction like this, although I'm sure there are less dramatic examples. It is the one that sticks in my mind far more powerfully than all the times when I may have done my job well. I don't want to forget it.

This is my job, but it applies to all of us in every area of our lives. Not recognizing physical cues, or recognizing them and reacting before pausing anyway, is not only unpleasant, it is dangerous. Whether it's road rage or an angry marital dispute, the compulsion to act on powerful and angry emotions takes conflict to a level where people feel hopeless, cornered, and desperate. We don't need to beat ourselves up for natural physiological reactions to threats or fear, but we can practice living with the discomfort before choosing a response to the discomfort.

Learning to Laugh at Ourselves

Embracing discomfort is never easy. But there are things we can do to help us through it. I remember an occasion when I began to realize the importance of laughing while experiencing personal conflict. It was around eight o'clock in the evening, and I was with some friends in our church basement. There were several chairs scattered around the room, scraping softly against the yellow vinyl floors as fifteen or twenty people mingled about, catching up.

Across the room, I saw my buddy Paul slumped down in a chair, leaning over the table in front of him, head in his hands. Paul was forty-five at the time, a skilled tool and die maker with a wife and two kids. He had a thin brown mustache and strong hands, and I always thought of him as a careful and purposeful person with a soft, slow voice that put others at ease.

On this night, he was different. Rather than slow and steady and reliable, he looked dazed. He stared vacantly, not participating in the chatter peppering the room. Struck by this stark contrast with the man I'd known for years, I walked over and pulled up a seat beside him.

"You don't look so good," I said. "Something must be up."

I wasn't prepared for his response.

"My wife kicked me out," he said, his usually soft-spoken nature betrayed by the strain in his voice. "My son refuses to talk to me, and my daughter told me she doesn't want to see me."

My heart went out to my friend, and I searched for something meaningful to say.

"So…something is definitely up."

Paul lifted his head, shooting me a wry smile. "Definitely."

"How's your wife handling it?"

Paul shrugged, then straightened his shoulders. "No idea," he said. "I may not be much, but I'm all I think about."

Paul's honesty startled a laugh out of a few friends within earshot, myself included. Suddenly, the sadness that had been hanging over him like a cloud lightened, ever so slightly, and he joined in with the laughter.

Of course, in the moment, Paul wasn't trying to be deep or philosophical, but he'd uncovered an indisputable truth about one of the paradoxes of being human: *I may not be much, but I'm all I think about.* All of us are susceptible to self-absorption in times of struggle. We care more about ourselves than anyone else, as if we are unique in our suffering. It's easy to get lost in self-analysis and mired down by circumstances, leaving us feeling hopeless, tense, and humorless. Learning to be self-aware without becoming self-absorbed can actually allow for lighthearted moments of self-discovery to emerge and a humorous perspective to develop, both of which help to release the pressure valve on conflict.

There was nothing to laugh about in Paul's difficult personal situation. But even as his internal conflict raged, his recognition that he was flawed and totally self-absorbed offered an admission that everyone could relate to. Accepting his painful reality allowed him a moment of levity, and instead of wallowing, he found the humor in it and gave in to the healing power of laughter. His raw admission connected him to everyone else in the room.

Paul's wise observation and the courage to share it pulled him out of isolation. He unknowingly invited all of us in, and we could laugh with him rather than run from his pain. We all know that scared and lonely feeling of unhelpful self-absorption in the face of what feels like overwhelming circumstances. Knowing people can share it and accept us in all our conflicted disarray is a place from which hope can spring.

Pain is not the normal path to laughter, but sometimes the best path is not the most natural one. The search for material solutions to immaterial problems plagues us all, and avoidance and denial are compelling, particularly if we feel alone and hopeless. However, accepting some responsibility for the conflict is one of the surest ways to find relief. And the ability to laugh at oneself is a powerful antidote to conflict, particularly the internal kind. Amazingly, it can connect us to others, who can help us climb out of the pit of paralyzing fear. Hearing a person whose defense mechanisms have been stripped away in a rare moment of candor can feel like the unexpected punchline of a great comic. Paul offered a glimpse of accidental good humor and insight. Unless he chose to, he would not be forced to face his conflict alone.

Practice Makes ... Better and Maybe Permanent

When we play a song on the piano and hit a wrong note, it sounds bad. Harmony is broken, and it hurts our ears. We know something must change, and we know it's not the composer's notes that need to change, but rather how we play them. Why can we know this so clearly when it comes to music and miss it so regularly with relationships? We easily accept that it takes practice to play a musical instrument, and that it is us who need to change when we hit a sour note, but not so much when we face the interior and exterior conflicts of life that confront us each day.

Practicing conflict is not an easy concept to swallow. There is a tendency to think that if we recognize something, a problem is solved—the intended result should just happen, not require painful practice. But we kid ourselves to think that conflict can be addressed without discomfort. It takes practice, and in the process we will hit more wrong notes—maybe even different ones. But without a change in ourselves (the only kind of change we can control), disharmony and pain will continue. The truth is that it hurts to hit wrong notes, and it hurts to practice different behavior.

It is also important to remember that practice is likely to "make permanent" whether it makes perfect or not, so paying attention to how and what you practice is important because it has consequences. We may need outside help to change the music or how we practice it.

Let's consider two responses to conflict that we can practice. If we are aware that we are in conflict, we can practice responding, just as we might practice the piano, yoga, or bowling. The two related areas are focus and gratitude.

Daniel Kahneman won the Nobel Prize for Economic Sciences in 2002. You can read about his story and his research in an engaging book, *Thinking, Fast and Slow*, published in 2011.[6] In one section of his book, Kahneman discusses the "focusing illusion." In short, Kahneman claims:

"Nothing in life is as important as you think it is when you are thinking about it."

One of Kahneman's gifts is to ask great questions and research them. He asks two different questions when considering the focusing illusion:

1. "How much pleasure do you get from your car?"

2. "What percentage of the day do paraplegics spend in a bad mood?"

Kahneman does some experimenting that I will not cover in detail beyond his conclusions. What he finds is that the pleasure from a car is most important when we think about it. We are likely to overvalue our pleasure from the car compared with the reality of the pleasure we get from it. There is a practical reason for our limited pleasure, and it has nothing to do with the car itself. Most of the time we are in the car, we are not thinking about the car because we focus on other things. We listen to the radio, talk to the person next to us, watch the countryside pass by, or daydream about a problem at work. If we are not paying attention to it, then we are not getting enjoyment from it.

Similarly, many long-term bad conditions do not consistently negatively affect us in the moment. We acclimate and focus on other things. Kahneman found that after a period of time (as little as a month in some cases), people who had become paralyzed enjoyed the routine activities of life such as working, reading, and spending time with friends as much as those who were not paralyzed.

---

6 Daniel Kahneman, *Thinking, Fast and Slow* (New York: Farrar, Straus and Giroux, 2011).

In those moments of deep engagement in things other than their paralysis, there was no difference in satisfaction. Most long-term states, whether marriage or paralysis, impact us primarily when we focus on them. They affect people "only when one attends to them."[7]

This is not the choice to avoid or deny. It is a conscious choice that accepts reality and chooses not to overvalue pleasures or over-invest in pain. It is the choice of thoughtful proportionality and acceptance. That is not to say that a car lover does not enjoy her car or someone who is paralyzed does not suffer. It is to say that, with some exceptions, we adapt and are well served to be aware of how we focus.

Some other scientists studied a specific focus—gratitude. Joel Wong and his research partner, Joshua Brown, study gratitude. Dr. Wong is a psychologist, and Dr. Brown is an engineer and neuroscientist. They are both professors at Indiana University. Dr. Wong once summarized their study by saying, "We got a grant to study gratitude, and learned that what your grandmother always told you is true…gratitude works." Gratitude is the practice of focusing on those things for which you are grateful. It seems simple, but it takes practice and has positive lasting effects.[8]

Wong and Brown studied students who were seeking mental-health counseling. They put students in three randomized groups. Members of one group wrote a gratitude letter each week, but they were not required to send it. Another group wrote about their deepest thoughts and feelings about negative experiences. A third group did no writing exercise.

The majority of the students in the study presented with issues

---

7   Kahneman, *Thinking*, 402–5.
8   Joel Wong and Joshua Brown, "How Gratitude Changes You and Your Brain," *Greater Good Magazine*, June 6, 2017, https://greater-good.berkeley.edu/article/item/how_gratitude_changes_you_and_your_brain.

of depression and anxiety. At the end of the study, the researchers made four findings:[9]

1. Gratitude unshackles us from toxic emotions.

2. Gratitude helps, even if you don't share it.

3. Gratitude's benefits take time.

4. Gratitude has lasting effects on the brain.

When we focus on the negative effects of conflict, that focus will take on a disproportionate and unhelpful role. We are fortunate if we have a safe and trusted person to share our rage with in moments of extreme conflict. And good friends or colleagues might help us to put the conflict in context. But one response that we may resist or not even think of is to be grateful for things other than conflict. The science suggests that focusing on things we are grateful for can help us balance our frustrations—not magically, but over time and with practice.

To make sure we are not relying on magic, Kahneman noted that there are exceptions to the focusing illusion: chronic pain, constant exposure to loud noise, and severe depression.[10] These three conditions generally do not allow our bodies to adapt, and therefore often transcend efforts to focus differently or practice gratitude. No matter how hard we try, we may need professional assistance, and this is another place for people we trust to offer perspectives that we are unable to get on our own.

---

9   Wong and Brown, "Gratitude."
10   Kahneman, *Thinking*, 405.

Final Thoughts on Discomfort

A note for those readers feeling discouraged by this massive undertaking of embracing discomfort: it's OK to feel that way. If you are consistently able to suspend advocating for your view of fairness, you are one of the few. Even if you manage it at times, it will not happen every time. Remember that you are human. Your willingness to embrace the discomfort of conflict and open yourself to someone who disagrees with you is a big commitment. Just as you will play wrong notes while practicing the piano, you will make mistakes engaging in conflict. The biggest mistake, however, may be in not engaging it.

Remember also that your principles and sense of fairness are important. Commitment to living your principles will allow you to hold your head high. However, stepping into a conflict by claiming the virtue and primacy of your principles over someone else's will inflame conflict.

Once you've decided you can live with putting your sense of fairness in perspective, you're ready to embrace discomfort. What's next? Read on to learn the second step in effectively engaging conflict: radical listening.

Takeaway

Embracing discomfort is an act of courage, though we may not naturally link the two. It requires us to face the reality of our choices, which can be a scary concept. There are times when pain and discomfort are mandatory. Making a choice to step into the fear instead of running from it, denying it, or fantasizing about it is an act of personal commitment, integrity, and accepting life on life's terms.

Action

When you feel your heart rate rise at an insult or "ridiculous" claim of someone else, before responding take a moment and consider what it would look like to be grateful—for the fact that you understand what the other person is saying, or for the fact that they do not have control over you, or that you live in a place where people can openly disagree. Ask whether a response is necessary. Then don't respond and see if your heart rate slows or your angry rebuttal is easier to let go of. Try it more than once to test the results of your practice.

11

Listening Radically

Listening radically is setting aside my agenda and being open to the possibility that I may be wrong...and *you* may be right. It is listening to someone else for the sole purpose of making every effort to understand them without preparing to debate them or change their minds. It is not natural, and it is hard, particularly in conflict.

Think about why you would *not* radically listen. What are you afraid of? Throughout the book, we've discussed the big fears of losing security, esteem, control, or comfort. Fear is a prime motivator, but as we discussed in the chapter on fear, it diminishes our ability to hear and see and be open to other possibilities when we're in conflict. Naturally we don't want to be hurt, embarrassed, rendered helpless, or made uncomfortable. And while we need to pay attention to these fears, we need not be totally driven by them. Instead, if we can learn to listen radically, we will learn things that we could not have imagined otherwise and find we can be OK in circumstances that threaten to paralyze us with fear.

Still, listening is no easy task. Consider this the next time you're chatting with friends or family members over a contentious topic—

whether it's politics, movies, or favored sports teams. As you each make your argument, notice how the conversation shifts. You may notice one person pausing in a show of respect for the other's argument, but the pause is quickly followed by the other person making her case for why she is right. Her counterpart may offer a reciprocal pause to listen. But this listening is not open to the possibility that she is mistaken. Instead, it is an exercise to look for any weak spot and criticize the other person in the fray. Both invariably lean on selective facts and "superior" logic. After a time, the pauses often get shorter or disappear altogether as both sides, now more aggravated, stop listening altogether and talk over each other.

At this point, the relationship between the parties will influence what happens. If the argument is between family members or close friends, one party may go silent or even leave in an attempt to salvage the relationship before things devolve further. Colleagues and professionals with few emotional ties might not make the effort to save anything. In fact, they may show outright disdain and contempt. Their words and behaviors can be just as damaging as throwing stones.

Instead of giving in to the temptation of arguing, we must break the cycle. The rush is not as thrilling, but the outcome might be infinitely more rewarding. Because it is hard, we won't like it very well, and it will take practice. We will make mistakes, and we'll have opportunities to forgive ourselves and others.

What Radical Listening Looks Like

Listening radically is not the passive listening of putting on a favorite old album or turning on a mindless sitcom for background noise. It is making a sincere effort to hear everything the other person is saying—even when it's uncomfortable. To do that, we need to take the cotton out of our ears and put it in our mouths. Because when we are talking, we are always missing something that someone else is saying. We *can't* talk and listen at the same time.

We think we multitask, but we don't. Even as we prepare to talk, we miss some or all of what is being said. We are afraid that we might forget something that needs to be corrected or responded to. We probably will, and we and others will be OK. My experience has been that no person, organization, or circumstance has unilaterally failed because I kept my thoughts to myself and listened to someone else's.

Your only response when listening radically is what the other person can see by your behavior—you are focused exclusively on them and what they are saying. It feels scary, like you are holding back some deep truth that the world (or at least the other person) needs to hear. All I can say is the world and other people function just fine without most of our "truths." When the other person is done talking, you can surrender to silence or say "thank you" and patiently wait to see what happens next.

Listening—especially the kind I'm advocating here—relinquishes the illusion that we can control what others think. We give up that control in order to open ourselves to someone else's agenda. The unimaginable might happen: someone else might have a better idea than ours. We also need to understand that this approach does not require reciprocity. The other person may not respond with the same kind of radical listening. If that's the case, try to remember that it's not a contest. Besides, if neither of you does it, then moving beyond the surface of conflict is impossible. Another listening do is being aware of our nonverbal communication. By consciously resisting the urge to mirror the other person's combative posture and adopting a peaceful one instead we can sometimes diffuse a heated conflict. Radical listening also means quieting our own internal conflicts and just showing up during difficult times. By employing various techniques of radical listening, we might hear important truths, salvage broken relationships, and work through conflict in a productive and meaningful way that on our own would have been impossible.

Listening without Demand

Our own thoughts are very important...to us. It doesn't feel natural to quiet our beliefs and opinions and simply *hear* someone else. We make a sacrifice when we squelch our instinct to interrupt. And you may feel after a radical-listening session that you are owed the same service in return. After all, to hear and not be heard goes against all our notions of fairness, and it makes our justice gene grit its teeth. It's natural to think you're entitled to a little quid pro quo. You are not. There is no scorekeeping in radical listening. Entitlement is not part of this equation, and it is a conflict aggravator. If you force the issue, you run the risk of undoing any positive progress you might have made.

There is also no expiration date on the "closed mouth, open ears" approach. No timer buzzes, giving you control of the playing field. It is not a courtroom trial in which one attorney makes a statement and then turns it over to the opposing side. If you're expecting reciprocity in radical listening, you're missing the point.

Even when someone wrongfully blames me, I can let them finish and make a genuine effort to understand before I defend and launch an attack back at them. I can own the responsibility for my inability (unwillingness?) to understand. I can accept when I don't understand. I can be compassionate toward their perspective, which might be diametrically opposed to my own. If I'm at my best, I might even be able not to blame them, not to ask them to change, and not tell them all the ways that they are wrong and I am right.

Though the demand for reciprocity feels reasonable, any demand for it makes conflict worse. If we can listen without making any demands, we reduce our self-focus and increase our vulnerability. This creates an environment where trust may be possible. Radical listening, which is *not* followed by immediate questioning or demands to have our side heard, can lower resistance and expose paths previously unseen by anyone, guiding us toward a more meaningful approach to conflict. Sometimes ceding power, which is not intuitive, can help.

Reciprocating Radically

Reciprocity is related to but different from mirroring. Mirroring often happens unconsciously when people are together, whether it is just two people talking over a cup of coffee or twenty people meeting in a conference room. If you pay attention, you will notice that as one person crosses their arms, another may do the same thing without realizing it. Mirroring happens with yawns, folded hands, and other gestures.

Reciprocity is more conscious than mirroring, but perhaps not completely so. If someone smiles at me, I'm likely to smile back. If I open the first of two doors for a stranger, the stranger may open the second door for me. If I buy lunch one day, my colleague may buy it the next. Reciprocity often flows naturally, but generally there is some awareness to it. We are particularly wired to mirror and reciprocate in cooperative environments. It lets people know that we are part of the group.

Reciprocity also happens negatively. If someone talks to me disrespectfully, I'm more inclined to be disrespectful in return. If someone interrupts me midsentence, I feel more at ease to interrupt them. If someone ignores me, I ignore them. If someone hogs the credit for a project, I may call them out or hog credit for the next one. This type of reciprocity is consistent with the justice gene, which operates to enforce our personal perception of what is fair. When we are in a conflict and someone pushes for their "unfair" fairness, the inclination is to push back...reciprocally. If one side or the other pushes too hard, the conflict escalates, sometimes beyond recovery, and then we are stuck with the most basic kind of conflict resolution—power against power. If that happens, you'd better be sure that you have correctly gauged your power and theirs.

Radically listening opens the door for you to choose another type of reciprocity: unconventional reciprocity. Unconventional reciprocity is really not reciprocating at all. It is a conscious choice not to respond in kind to negative behavior. It is the choice not to embarrass when embarrassed, not to hurt feelings when yours have been hurt, not to even the score when someone has behaved unfairly. It is not a natural choice, and it is not always the best choice, but it can be a helpful choice.

A good example of someone choosing to engage in a conflict using unconventional reciprocity is Cicely, the lawyer we talked about in chapter 3. When the other lawyer in the mediation case she was involved in went to court to get an emergency order without properly notifying her, she felt like she had been treated unfairly and disrespectfully. When she considered calling out the other lawyer, she decided it would get in the way of her goal of trying to settle the case for her client. She paused and chose not to reciprocate negatively.

A basketball coach on the receiving end of negative reciprocity was able to break the cycle of tit for tat by choosing unconventional reciprocity instead. Louise coached a middle-school girls' basketball team. She ran a tight ship and drew clear lines between the role of an adult coach and that of teenaged players. She maintained a defined chain of command and expected to be treated respectfully by her players.

One day during practice, Louise called out her backup point guard, Maddie, for a repeated shortcoming in her play.

"Doggone it, Maddie!" Louise yelled. "You've done the same darned thing three times down the floor."

"Well, Louise," Maddie yelled back, calling her by name instead of "Coach," "maybe you need to stop screaming at me and find another backup."

The rest of the girls froze in their tracks, wondering what Louise would do as Maddie ran into the locker room. Louise was ready to run after Maddie and yell at her to get back right now. But she didn't.

Maddie's words and behavior violated all of Louise's expectations. Radically listening also involves watching behavior, and Maddie's outburst was not normal for her, so much so that Louise held off from her usual coach's reaction of yelling at Maddie and giving her some sort of penalty for disrespectful behavior. It wasn't so much that Louise condoned Maddie's behavior; it was more that she instinctively realized that her typical reaction to demand respect might not be the best one to fall back on in a situation that surprised her.

Louise told the other players to continue their scrimmage and followed Maddie into the locker room, where she was sitting on a bench sobbing. Empathy was not Louise's natural response to her players, but she was capable of summoning it. It was clear that this wasn't the time to exert her power over Maddie, and she was able to set aside her rigid coaching approach.

Louise sat down next to Maddie and put her hand on her shoulder without saying a word. Maddie's shoulders slowly stopped heaving, and her breathing returned to normal. Louise continued to sit there quietly.

Finally, after several minutes, Maddie said, "I'm sorry. Can I go back to practice now?"

Louise waved her back to the gym without requiring an explanation.

Later that evening, Louise learned that Maddie's parents had told her and her sisters that morning that they were moving to another state at the end of the month. A difficult life change for anyone, but maybe especially for kids. In a moment of radical listening, radical empathy, and an uncharacteristic willingness not to demand an explanation, Louise was able to show Maddie a bit of kindness by choosing not to reciprocate negatively, even though Maddie broke the rules. At least as surprising, Louise did not explain the departure in her own behavior to the team. She gave them a chance to figure it out for themselves, which was its own kind of respect for them.

Radical listening is an act of compassion.

If you are feeling threatened or dismissed, radical listening is a rebellious response because it breaks the cycle of negative reciprocity. It tests whether incremental acts of generosity might instead spark positive reciprocity and lower the overall temperature of the conflict from near boiling to something only uncomfortably warm. Radical listening offers a counterintuitive willingness to be open and kind even in the face of harsh criticisms or insults. It refuses to mirror the anger, righteousness, and fear that inform every conflict. Radical listening in the midst of conflict does not guarantee that the other side will reciprocate with generosity, but it does create an environment that makes that connection possible.

Invest in Someone Else's Agenda

Radical listening is an investment in the other person—in what they say, how they feel, and the value they bring to the relationship. It is nearly always uncomfortable, frequently awkward, and sometimes terrifying. And it requires that we expend the effort to act on it. If you do it, if you open yourself to the other person's agenda, you will be vulnerable. If you don't do it, the conflict is nearly guaranteed to escalate. In a more fundamental sense, radically listening is being kind.

When our three daughters were small, we would pack them into our red Taurus station wagon and go to a cabin in Lake Charlevoix, Michigan. It was about a nine-hour drive, depending on how many stops we made. I always liked to get up and on the road at dawn because I enjoyed driving while the girls were sleeping and we could arrive at the cabin while it was still daylight. It was more comfortable for me, and I imposed my process on everyone else.

My wife, Patty, did almost all the packing and preparation. Those of you who have traveled with young children understand all of the stuff they require: portable cots and cribs, high chairs, swim gear, toys, and much more. Patty did the pre-trip preparation every single time. While I turned in early to get up early for the drive, Patty stayed up late packing to make sure we had everything we needed. It's not a news flash that Patty didn't enjoy waking up early to get on the road after having packed well into the night.

There was nothing wrong with either of our approaches to prepping for our vacation, and yet we both felt frustration and resentment brewing in the days leading up to our trips. Why couldn't Patty prepare earlier? I would think. Why did she wait until the last minute? At the same time, she was wondering why I never offered to help—and why I went to bed while she was still up working. Each year, we could feel this tension looming as we approached our departure date. Still, I had my agenda: get plenty of sleep and be well rested to ensure an easy drive north. Changing the schedule—or helping out with the packing—would require me to listen to something that challenged that agenda or to take instruction on how to pack.

My agenda—to nourish my own comfort—was not the most important element of a successful family vacation. This vacation was not about me. In fact, I—all of us, really—can use that same framework for nearly any situation. "This fight is not about you." "This party is not about you." "This disappointment is not about you." How many conflicts would be resolved if we could recognize "This _____ is not about you"?

Our challenge is that we only experience conflict through ourselves and we validate our own common sense, our own point of view, and our own comfort. There is no listening to or understanding someone else. If challenged, we may find our first response is to defend our way and explain why it is better than the alternative.

Before we returned from the lake, I set aside my agenda and asked what she needed to feel better about our travel plans. I began to accept that things could be done in a different way…even when it wasn't *my* way. And that, believe it or not, even if we didn't set out at the crack of dawn, the world would keep on spinning. I want to be careful here. It's not as if I should get credit for doing something one time that I should have been doing for years. But what I learned by radically listening to Patty is that it also felt good not to be so entitled and to make life easier for someone I loved.

I had refused to hear Patty's needs because doing that would mean I would have to stop arguing for mine. I would have to stop thinking about my own comfort and instead think of hers. I would have to shut my mouth and open my ears. Sounds easy, but it's not.

Our girls are adults now, so the family vacations operate a little differently. Patty and I still have our individual travel preferences, but we also have an open and honest dialogue about our expectations, needs, and desires so, instead of dreading an upcoming trip, we can feel excited and look forward to the time we'll spend together and the memories we'll make. We both get to be generous and not focus on our own preferences, which makes life so much better.

Setting aside our own agenda is essential to being able to listen radically. In doing this, we accept what the other side is saying without argument. We choose to believe that *they* believe what they're saying, even if we disagree. It is not a time for correction or argument. Not only do we have to be OK with hearing that we're wrong, we also have to be OK facing the evidence that we actually *are* wrong. This approach is just as beneficial in meetings with my partners or anyone else. It is a choice and it takes practice.

Accept Uncertainty

When I am most uncomfortable or fearful, I search high and low for control. Denial of the reality of uncertainty feels like a comfortable landing spot, but only because I cannot see the flimsy legs on which it rests. I grasp for Option F—fantasy. Sometimes radical listening starts with admitting that I just don't know what to do in a circumstance I cannot control.

Jim and I had been friends for a couple of years when he was diagnosed with prostate cancer. Although he was only sixty years old and seemed otherwise healthy, by the time his cancer was discovered it had spread to his bones. The doctors did not tell him how long he would live, but they did tell him to get his affairs in order.

Jim had retired to Bloomington from Washington, DC, where he had worked with federal law enforcement. He was a slight man with big opinions and many experiences to relate. He loved being around people and was deeply grateful for his life. It was easy for a quick cup of coffee with Jim to stretch into a couple of hours of listening to stories. He and his wife, Ethel, had saved their money and planned to enjoy their retirement for many years. They looked forward to doing things that they had put off until now.

Over the course of six months, Jim's condition deteriorated rapidly. He spent his last few weeks in hospice care, confined to a hospital bed in the home that he and Ethel had made for themselves.

During this time, I went to visit Jim weekly. Jim spent his days resting in the back bedroom. He knew he was going to die, but that didn't stop him from enjoying the birds at the feeders outside the window or watching the fall colors begin to paint the trees. There was a TV set up at the foot of the bed and a chair for guests. It was as peaceful and comfortable as his family could make it.

I was always uncomfortable when I went to see Jim. I prefer to say "uncomfortable," but I was really *afraid*—of my own powerlessness to help, of my own death, of not knowing what to say, and of wondering if Jim even cared that I was there. I wanted to rationalize that I didn't matter so I would have an excuse not to go. My internal conflict over wanting to avoid my own fears around seeing a friend die and wanting to be a good friend kicked into high gear. Still, I went.

One crisp autumn morning I showed up just as Jim awoke. He nodded a greeting but closed his eyes and didn't say anything. Unable or unwilling to be still or stay silent, I got busy. Jim was the one with terminal cancer, and yet I was the one who was jumpy and ill at ease. Have you ever noticed how empty busyness can be a cover for powerlessness? I fluffed his pillow, turned on the TV, and carried some dirty dishes to the kitchen.

When I came back, I started asking questions.

"Is there anything I can get you?"

"How are you feeling?"

"Did you sleep OK?"

"Is the pain tolerable?"

"Want me to read something to you?"

"Did you watch the Cubs?"

I didn't pause for Jim to answer, I just pattered on.

Jim didn't respond. Finally, with great effort, he turned slowly toward me, raised his head off the pillow, and said, "Will you just sit down, be quiet, and hold my hand?"

Against all my instincts, I surrendered to Jim's request. I sat down on the chair and quietly held Jim's hand until he fell asleep.

Jim died about a week later. "Sit down, be quiet, and hold my hand" are the last words he said to me.

When faced with someone else's pain and uncertainty, it is easy to want to deny our own powerlessness and to avoid our own pain and uncertainty. I loved Jim, but because his cancer and condition scared me, I thought I had to *do something* to help and to distract myself from thoughts about my own mortality. I reacted to my feelings of fear by looking for a place where I could have an impact. I'd have told you that it was to help Jim, and of course that was what I wanted. But ultimately, it was more about helping myself. The one thing I could do—stop resisting and accept the uncertainty—was the last thing that occurred to me. My empty busyness required energy from a dying man just to get me to be quiet. I couldn't see until much later that the most powerful gift I could offer was to remain quietly present and not run from my own fear while Jim lived with his.

Drop the Bottle (and the Insanity)

When it became clear, even to me, that I needed to quit drinking, I called a friend for help. He had a long history of drinking and an even longer history of staying sober. He invited me to his house to talk. We went onto his back porch, and almost before we sat down, he began talking.

"You have to make sobriety the most important thing in your life, because unless you make it your highest priority, you will lose everything. Maybe even your life." He looked me dead in the eye.

I knew I needed to stop drinking, but I was not prepared for such an unvarnished approach.

"I want your help, but I'm not sure I'm ready for you to set my priorities for me right off the bat," I responded nervously.

"If what you're doing is working, then why are you here talking to me?" He looked like he was ready to get up.

The short conversation scared me. I didn't know where else to go. I was drinking nearly a quart of vodka every day. I couldn't *not* drink. It was like he could read my mind.

"Alcoholism is first and foremost a disease of self-deception," he told me. "I'll bet you get up lots of mornings, sure that you won't drink, and by the time the day ends you pass out drunk."

"You're right," I said. "But I have a lot going on. I know I need to stop drinking, but making sobriety my number one priority may be a bit much."

I felt like I was getting my argumentative sea legs under me, so I went on, searching for the exception. I felt ready to push back.

"If someone is holding my wife and daughters hostage and threatens to kill them unless I drink, then I'm going to drink," I said, pleased with myself.

He took a long moment and then leaned forward in his chair.

"If that happens, Sam," he said, "then you go ahead and drink."

No one said anything for what seemed like an eternity.

"Is that it?" I asked.

"It is unless you want to do something different," he said.

Even though my intense internal conflict had driven me to call him in the first place and ask him for help, the minute he told me something that I didn't want to hear, I grabbed the rope and wanted to play tug-of-war with him. He dropped the rope, unwilling to play. It threw me off balance and robbed me of any satisfaction in my smug reply.

My friend's response was brilliant. He was clear that if I was determined to continue to reach my own conclusions, then he had nothing to offer me. He radically listened to me and allowed me the complete freedom to believe I could still figure it out. He did not try to convince me I was wrong. He did not run from the conflict I was inviting, he just refused to participate in it. He shifted the responsibility to me and did not feel any compunction to control my future behavior.

And by simply refusing to engage in my silly game, my friend defused the conflict with hardly a word. I couldn't be mad at him for agreeing with me, could I? But how could he agree with something so absurd? Actually, he wasn't agreeing with me. He just told me I had the freedom to base my decisions on a ridiculous exception…or not. He did not agree to solve my problem for me, and he made it much more difficult for me to deny it. He was sober; I wasn't. I wanted to argue, and I didn't want to change. A painless choice was unavailable.

He very skillfully allowed me to experience the anxiety of my own foolhardiness. He refused to take on my anxiety, and in doing so made it harder for me to run from it. Giving me the freedom to reach my own conclusion was far more powerful than engaging in my outlandish argument.

The exchange with my friend was brief, but it revealed a huge flaw in my own thinking that was literally killing me. It also showed me that if we allow people the freedom to face and own their own failure, even if that failure is catastrophic, we have a greater chance

to influence them. This approach does not guarantee a specific result to a conflict, but it is much more likely to create an environment for a productive interaction.

After allowing me a few minutes to process, he must have
thought I could hear him, and he became more direct.

"Sam, if you asked the next teenager coming out of White Castle what you should do next, their advice would be more reliable
than your own thinking is right now."

In a moment of clarity, I abandoned defensiveness and radically
listened in return, even though I had never thought of the concept.
I showed up thinking that I might have a drinking problem, but
that I could curate my way through it to keep doing what I was
doing and also stop or slow my drinking. Some people can do that;
I was just not one of them. Sometimes it takes a revelation from
someone else to remove the scales from our eyes, allowing us to
radically listen. With practice, I think we can learn to do it without
going to such depths.

I believed my friend was being arrogant, and maybe oppressive,
when he told me what my first priority must be. He listened carefully, but refused to take the bait I offered to use conflict to deflect
from the point. His wisdom was in refusing to have the argument.
He did not interfere with my freedom to reach my own misguided
conclusions. He never said that I had to do or understand anything.
If I really thought my way was working, I had every right to continue. He showed a curious mix of confidence in his beliefs and an
acceptance of his powerlessness to control me. He did not push his
agenda, but he listened carefully and asked the right questions.

Who Asked You?

Radical listening is an effort to dedicate all of our senses to
seeing, hearing, feeling, and understanding what the other person is
trying to communicate. It is not looking for an opportunity to give
advice or redirect the focus onto ourselves.

Abe and his sister, Esther, could not agree on how to support their aging parents, who didn't want to move from their home. The last time Esther visited there, she drove up just as her ninety-two-year-old father slipped on ice as he was shoveling snow off the walkway. Her eighty-eight-year-old mother wouldn't have been able to hear his yells for help from inside the house, and Esther hated to think about what would have happened had she not been there.

Abe asked if I'd be willing to have a cup of coffee and just listen to what was going on. We met at a local coffee joint.

"Esther and I both want what's best for our parents, but we can't agree on what that is," Abe began. "They're physically challenged, but they're both thinking OK. Esther wants to move them to a safer place. Even though I'm scared they might get hurt, I'm willing to support them to stay in their house because it seems like they have that right. Esther is probably right that they'd be safer in a retirement home, and she's mad at me for not supporting her on that. We all take risks, and I'm willing to let them continue to choose their risks, even getting on ladders, if that's what they want."

Abe's words began to run together.

"It seems to me—"

"Golly, what a hard situation," I interrupted. "We went through the same thing with my parents, and it was really hard to decide what to do."

Abe tried to continue with his thoughts, but I raised my voice over his just enough that he allowed me to continue.

"I'll bet you and Esther have really struggled with..."

I stopped as I looked at Abe, who had folded his hands in his lap and was just staring at me.

"What?" I asked, unsure what his body language meant.

"All I asked you to do was listen," Abe said. "Before I could even finish my story, you began telling yours, and it sounds like you're about ready to tell me what to do. You offered to listen and then made it all about you."

We both sat there awkwardly. I could hear Abe breathing.

"You're right," I apologized. "I have no defense. Please go on and I'll shut up."

Abe and I had known each other for a long time. Long enough for him to interrupt me right back and point out that not only had I not radically listened, I had barely listened at all. I had hijacked the conversation to relate my own similar story. He stopped me before I could offer a solution he had not requested. I was embarrassed but grateful for Abe's candor.

Suggestions are frequently well-intentioned but less often desired or requested. And they might only cause more suffering to someone who is uncertain or afraid. I am not saying that we don't sometimes have wise counsel to offer, but unless we have the most intimate kind of relationship, unsolicited advice is rarely welcomed and seldom solves a problem…except the problem of our desire to be relevant or important. We may be far more relevant by holding our tongues.

Remember, listening is its own thing. Once you open your mouth, listening is over. Interjecting your own story is your way of controlling the situation by solving someone else's problem…even if they didn't ask you to. When you add dialogue, it's now a conversation. And while conversations can be helpful and rewarding, they are not always what's needed. When we feel compelled to jump in with our own experience or advice, thinking we're being helpful, in reality we're simply communicating impatience, lack of concern, and self-centeredness. This kind of "help," however pure the motives, will not build connections.

Of course, not everyone does this. But for me, it is a defining character flaw. Giving suggestions for some of us is natural, whether they are wanted or not. When we feel powerless and the potential consequences are significant, offering advice gives us a sense of control. We might not recognize this kind of advice giving as a power play, but any effort to influence shows a desire for power as we attempt to make our illusion of control become reality. It is another response to fear.

On the other hand, when someone does ask for advice, we can choose to offer it or not. If we choose to advise, we'd better be generous and understanding if the advice is not followed.

Even with a special or close relationship, our suggestions are not always welcomed. It is true even when parenting our own children. A counselor friend once said that the biggest points of conflict between teenagers and parents occur when parents "answer the questions that have not been asked." Guilty!

Radically listening with the humble purpose of doing nothing more than trying to understand is a generous gift.

Takeaway

Radical listening is an act of compassion to make the other person comfortable instead of making yourself comfortable. It requires the sincere effort to listen with the goal of understanding, not responding. Radical listening creates a space for us to see things that would have escaped us if we were preparing to respond.

Action

The next time you are listening to someone, try these three things:

1. Allow a silence to continue until the other person says more, without you commenting, no matter how awkward you find the silence.

2. Don't voice points of disagreement, but attempt to understand why the other person feels the way they do.

3. After the conversation ends, pay attention to how you feel and whether you think you learned something you would have missed had you not radically listened.

12

Accepting Responsibility

Y ou have responsibility for any disagreement or conflict you are in. You may not have started it, but you decide whether to engage with it or leave it and how to participate if you do engage in it. Your conflicts simply cannot exist without you. You cannot have an *internal conflict* if you internalize and accept, without shame, the fact that you sometimes will not meet the expectations of yourself or others. You cannot have an *external conflict* if you accept the circumstances exactly as they are or the change as someone else wishes it to be.

As discussed in chapter 1, conflict arises whenever opposing forces or desires collide and cannot be readily reconciled. You are the common denominator in deciding what is or is not reconciled…for you. Someone else may remain in conflict after you have left it behind. If there is no response required and your fears are no longer tweaked, the conflict for you has ended. But it does not always seem so simple.

At this moment, you can probably remember a time when you chose not to respond. In chapter 9 we learned about Carlos and Lexi, who did not go to HR or hire a lawyer because they decided, after weighing all the options, that engaging external conflict was not their best choice. They avoided the external conflict but continued to assimilate the internal conflict they felt about how the circumstances *should be* different. Carlos's boss, Gus, did not seem to have a conflict. He was fine with his behavior, regardless of whether we think it was unacceptable.

Your internal conflict is always yours to work out, at least unless you decide that engaging it externally has value. Carlos could have confronted Gus, and then Gus would have had an external conflict. Carlos chose otherwise.

The justice gene never fully disappears, and it is important to keep in mind that there is no conflict for you without your participation, whether you are aware of it or not. You are the common thread—and the only one you can control—in all your conflicts.

Accepting responsibility is owning your part of the conflict. It does not always lead to agreement, but it establishes a possibility for one or both sides to do more than try to take something or defend something. It redirects the conversation from the endgame to the process and the relationship. Done effectively, it brings some humanity back into the game. You don't have to like the circumstances to accept responsibility for them, but you will know you have reached a point of acceptance if the physical symptoms we've discussed that accompany conflict begin to recede.

A Principled Disagreement

The novel coronavirus intermittently brought parts of the world to its knees in 2020. Different points of view about how to respond to the pandemic offered ample opportunities for people to engage in conflict. Sometimes the conflicts were the big-picture ones about how nations and communities should view and respond to the virus. Other times the conflicts were powerfully intimate ones about how people living in the same home should view and respond to the virus. I heard these stories countless times and was grateful that Patty and I responded fairly similarly in our own home. Some of our friends were not so fortunate. They suffered deep-seated and principled battles about how to achieve the same goal of keeping their families safe.

Duke and Minnie are friends who live in the Pacific Northwest, where the virus first got the most publicity in the United States. Duke is a building contractor, and Minnie is a landscape architect who works part-time and cares for their two elementary-aged children when she is not working. From the moment the virus was first identified, Duke wanted to take immediate action to protect their family. He agreed with the most ardent advocates of shutting down, maintaining social distance, washing hands, and wearing masks. Duke followed the news and social media and joined unofficial chat rooms. With each passing day, he became more and more concerned about the situation.

Minnie was unsure that the reports of the threat were accurate and was equally unsure where she could get reliable information to reach a conclusion. She was not unconcerned about the dangers, but she had a wait-and-see attitude.

Their conflict was framed by a disagreement as to how to respond. They struggled individually and collectively to sort through the very real conflict of how they could live their lives in the same household when they saw the threat of the circumstances so differently.

They sent me email asking if we could talk. Once I heard what they wanted to talk about, I reminded them that I was not a therapist and no longer did family mediations. They asked to talk anyway. Their emails to each other describe a long conversation that I'm summarizing here.

"Minnie," Duke wrote, "I've watched CNN, Fox, and MSNBC, read Facebook feeds, and visited the Centers for Disease Control website. All but Fox and maybe the CDC think all hell is going to break loose, and we need to be prepared."

Duke had reached the unassailable conclusion that their family needed to act right away and move to a remote cabin in the woods.

"Life seems to be going on just fine around here as far as I can see," Minnie responded. "They might cancel school, but they haven't yet. The kids seem to be fine, except when *you* get them stirred up. We both have lots of work to do here."

Minnie and Duke were equally committed to their marriage and the safety of their children. What were they to do when one saw a present threat that called for an immediate response and the other saw a possible threat that did not yet require an immediate response? They both thought that the other's response was unreasonable and that acting or not acting would be bad for the family for different reasons.

To go back to an earlier concept, Duke and Minnie each thought that they had just the right amount of common sense. That meant they thought the other was totally misguided about whether the virus was a big deal and the right way to respond to it.

After reading the email, I agreed to talk with them, provided that I would not weigh in on what they should do. We gathered via an online videoconferencing platform about a week later.

Patty and I had been friends with Minnie and Duke since before they were married, more than twenty years ago. The pain they were experiencing was palpable over two thousand virtual miles. I thought back to the day when Patty had asked me if I'd rather be right or I'd rather be married. The topic was so small that we cannot remember it, and Patty was making a point. Minnie and Duke were facing a much more existential threat, and they struggled with uncertainty and fear.

Minnie and Duke were on such opposite ends of the debate that they felt like they did not recognize the person they had married, and they both felt judged. Neither one could see any way to a compromise or any way to surrender to the other's point of view...because it was so clearly wrong!

After a few pleasantries, we began.

"You go ahead and start," Minnie said to Duke.

Duke took the offer without hesitation.

"We hate to involve you, Sam, but we just can't sort this out. We know that you can't tell either of us what to do, but we wanted an outside perspective."

"I'll do what I can," I said.

"There's just no way to see this coronavirus as anything but a threat to our family and the whole country," Duke said. "Minnie acts like there's nothing wrong, and she puts our kids in harm's way every single day when she sends them to school, takes them to the grocery store, and allows them to play with friends. It's not just the kids—she's risking the health of our whole family. We need to go one way or the other, because there's no way to compromise."

Duke took a breath, which opened a space for Minnie.

"I love Duke, and we both love our kids," Minnie said, offering an olive branch. "There is so much information out there that we have no ability to know who's telling us the truth. And this isn't just about the virus. I've never wanted to homeschool my kids, but that seems to be Duke's solution. People develop mental health problems from being isolated from family and friends, and that's the risk if we move to a cabin in the woods.

"Kids get depressed, and people hit each other and their children when they're kept away from outside friends and family. Plus, we aren't rich. We make enough money to pay our bills if we keep doing what we're doing. But if we totally isolate and don't work, it won't be long before our house is being foreclosed on. What then?"

The two of them stared at each other. They seemed more scared and frustrated than contemptuous, so there was a glimmer of hope.

Before Duke could respond, I interrupted.

"I've known you a long time, and you love each other and your children," I began. "Even though you couldn't disagree more about the virus, do either of you disagree that you both want what's best for your whole family and your marriage?"

"She can't want what's best if she keeps doing what she is doing," Duke said.

"Do you really believe that, Duke?" I asked before Minnie could answer.

"I guess not," Duke admitted.

Minnie was now leaning back instead of forward. She wisely did not respond to Duke's insult about maybe not caring about the family.

"None of us knows what's going to happen for sure," I continued, "but it's doubly hard when you're making decisions not only for yourselves but for your kids, too. That scares any parent. You feel like you have to get it right, and the two of you disagree what right is, even though you both care so much."

"Listen, I own the fact that I worry less than Duke. Sometimes I feel like I just hand my anxiety over to him so I don't have to think about it," Minnie said, almost smiling and changing the tone of the conversation. "When we go on vacation, Duke is so nervous about keeping everyone safe that he can hardly enjoy it. I appreciate that about him."

"Minnie would assume we'd be OK tied to the tracks with a train bearing down on us," Duke said. "That's OK when it's about eating junk food or watching TV, but this is life or death. I do worry too much, but that's because Minnie worries too little. Someone has to do it. I'd just feel so awful if something happened to anyone in our family, including Minnie."

"It's not like I don't care," Minnie responded a little defensively, "but just because we don't know the future doesn't mean the worst is going to happen. I love our kids too. We just feel so stuck. I hate feeling this way, and I'm mad at Duke, the virus, and myself all at once!"

"I know I'm part of the problem, here," Duke said. "I have no idea how to fix it, and I'd rather be safe than sorry."

There is a tendency in these circumstances to oversimplify and make a claim about what "the problem" is. Complex issues do not reduce themselves to a single problem, however, and despite their discomfort, neither Minnie nor Duke simplified the difficulty. They each accepted responsibility for some of the difficulty in having the conversation, and they agreed about their personal priorities. They agreed that they both loved their family and valued their marriage. They also expressed some appreciation for the other. Minnie complimented Duke when she said that she transfers her worry over to him and appreciates the burden he carries to keep everyone safe. Duke owned his worry and his frustration at the inability to fix the problem.

They did not yet have an answer about whether they both needed to compromise or either one needed to surrender. They agreed about priorities, but disagreed about what to do. So they began with some big-picture things that they did agree about. They loved their family and each other. They admitted that some of the ways they transferred responsibilities, including worry, often worked well, but not in this case. They also agreed that they were both afraid, but of different things.

Duke was afraid of the virus itself, and Minnie was afraid of the consequences of responding to the virus. They stopped trying to convince each other which of those fears made more sense. They respected their right to be afraid.

Minnie asked Duke for specifics on how to address his fears about getting the virus and the grave consequences to the health of the family. Duke listened to Minnie talk in more detail about her fears of the family being isolated. They stepped out of blaming each other and minimizing the other's fear. Having the conversation differently allowed them to remember that they were on the same team with the same concern.

Their ultimate conclusion was to talk to a couple of other families who were willing to become their own pods, with the same social-distancing, hygiene, and mask-wearing practices. They combined shopping trips, homeschooling, and social interaction to limit contact while staying socially engaged. They worked out ways for

Minnie and Duke to keep working and for the other two families in their group to do the same.

It was imperfect. Minnie was sometimes too casual for Duke, and Duke was sometimes too controlling for Minnie. They made mistakes, and the fear didn't magically disappear. But they muddled through and did their best to focus on the fact that everyone was doing their best to address a situation that none of them created. At the time of this writing, they have continued this approach for many months.

Almost any conflict that becomes intractable like Minnie and Duke's is impossible to positively engage in if the discussion revolves around disagreement about an exclusive way to the best outcome. If it stays there, the fear about a bad result demands all the attention. To step out of that and accept some responsibility is one path out of the impasse, but it nearly always requires someone to take a risk and be vulnerable. The other person can just as easily exploit our acceptance of responsibility as they can embrace it. That makes us vulnerable and is scary. But in most conflicts, we are scared anyway. And unless someone takes the risk, without a promise of the desired result, the fight is guaranteed to continue until someone just quits and leaves it to the fates.

At no time did I tell Minnie or Duke to accept responsibility. I asked some questions. They owned their part of the problem on their own once they took their focus away from the fear and reminded themselves of a common goal of caring for their family. The fear was not gone, but the focus on it was diminished, and the space was created for them to recover their breath.

Responsibility without Excuse: Different Lenses

Some disagreements seem purely legal when we lawyers get involved, but the solutions routinely involve much more than the law. The formalized process of a lawsuit can remove the humanity from an issue that always starts with basic human feelings. It is why these things are so challenging. The following story is an example.

Some people came to see me about settling a dispute between a woman who had invented a product and the president of the business that she licensed the patent to. The business began with a very personal relationship between the inventor and the owner of a small enterprise, which later grew into an international company. The company paid the inventor for years, but there was a disagreement about how long she would be paid. The company thought their obligation to pay her was over. The inventor thought the company should pay her indefinitely. Before the most recent dispute, the relationship between both parties had been good, and both had prospered from it.

Both sides could survive the outcome of the litigation, but the amount of money in question was significant. The inventor and the man who started the company both said that the conflict was a matter of principle.

When talking privately with the inventor's lawyer, he admitted that he believed that the law favored the company and not his client. He told me that I could not share that opinion.

As the mediation unfolded, the inventor and the president of the company both shared how the relationship had started. Donetta, the inventor, was just out of high school when she ran into Vern, the company president, at a convenience store in their small town. Vern had a tool and die shop and knew Donetta's parents. Donetta did not like school, but she did enjoy fiddling around in her dad's garage with leftover parts from cars. Her dad was an amateur mechanic. Donetta liked the way shocks worked and experimented with ways to make them absorb bumps more smoothly on bicycles. With her dad's help, she then applied her ideas to cars. Donetta's dad died before she graduated from high school, and she continued to work with her designs.

Donetta asked Vern if he could look at her ideas and maybe make the parts for her design. They came up with a plan, and Vern put Donetta in touch with a lawyer to apply for a patent. Donetta got the patent when she was only twenty years old. Vern agreed to license it to produce the shocks, which turned out to have a broad application.

They both made a lot of money. After nearly twenty years of payments, Vern felt that he had paid Donetta enough, and he decided to enforce the original twenty-year contract. Vern was ready to retire, and he wanted to resolve things with Donetta before stepping away.

Donetta had always thought that Vern got more than his fair share, and she never invented anything after this. They never signed anything beyond their original agreement. They wrote it themselves without lawyers.

The mediation started early in the morning. Late in the afternoon, we were nearing a place where everyone was ready to end the mediation and go try the case. I was wrapping it up but decided to visit each room once more.

"Donetta, did you ever see this coming?" I asked.

"Not really," she said. "Vern was friends with my dad. I thought he would pay me until one of us died. I trusted him to do what is fair."

"So, you thought Vern would pay you forever?"

"Maybe not forever," she said carefully. "I knew that we had a deal to end it at twenty years, but Vern made so much money, I assumed he'd continue to pay me."

"You're not really shocked, then?"

"I still am," she said. "We aren't lawyers, and I was young. Neither of us knew how successful this would be. Fair is all I want."

"Do you think Vern is unfair?" I asked.

"I didn't until he stopped paying me."

We talked for a few more minutes, and then I went to talk to Vern to see if there was any reason to continue.

"It looks like we may be done," I said to Vern and his lawyer. "I hate to give up. You and Donetta seemed to have gotten along for years. Is there anything we can do to settle this?"

"I don't know what," Vern said. "I've paid Donetta so much money, and all she did was invent one thing."

"Did you ever manufacture anything else that had this kind of success?"

"That isn't the point," Vern said, dodging my question. "A deal is a deal. It was for twenty years, and those twenty years are up."

"How old was Donetta when you made this agreement?"

"I don't know for sure," Vern said, "but in her early twenties."

"Did either of you use lawyers to write up the agreement?" I asked, knowing the answer.

"We avoided lawyers, except for the patent, and that was Donetta's," Vern said.

"How old were you when this started?" I asked.

"I think I'm about twenty years older, so somewhere in my forties," Vern answered. "Where is this going?"

"You and Donetta have said some similar things," I said. "Donetta said that she only wanted what was fair. You said 'a deal is a deal.' That sounds like you only want what's fair too. Am I right?"

"If you're asking about wanting what is fair, you're right," Vern said.

"Did you and Donetta have any problems before you stopped paying her?"

"No."

"Do you think she ever looked at the agreement before you sent her the letter telling her it was over?

"No idea."

"Do you know if she even had a copy?"

"Nope," Vern said, getting irritated with me.

"We're almost done, and settlement looks pretty bleak," I said, "If the lawyers agree, would you be willing to meet with just Donetta?"

"I hadn't planned on that." Vern said. "I need to talk with my lawyer without you."

I left the room and asked the same question of Donetta and her lawyer.

Both lawyers and both clients agreed for the two of them to talk. The lawyers asked that I be in the room but that I not direct the conversation. We agreed that it would end when either Vern or Donetta wanted it to.

Donetta, Vern, and I went into another conference room together. There was an awkward but short silence as they both looked at the floor. Vern and Donetta had not seen each other in years.

"I'm sorry," Vern began as he looked up. "This isn't what I wanted, but a deal is a deal. It was for twenty years." He said this firmly but not unkindly.

"I was twenty years old," Donetta said. "My dad had died, and I had no idea what I was signing. My lawyer told me today that you'd probably win at trial, and he told me not to tell you that. It's my own fault for not looking sooner. I just thought you'd pay me forever because you made so much money."

"It's not my fault that you didn't look at the contract," Vern stated, but he was a little taken aback by Donetta's honesty. He was also surprised that she admitted it was her fault for not looking sooner.

"I knew the contract was ending," Vern said. "I had a copy of the contract, and I knew it ended after twenty years. I should have called you to let you know ahead of time, but I was afraid this would happen. I thought by not saying anything, you'd look at the contract and agree with me. You're right, though—I did make a lot of money...and so did you."

Donetta was looking at Vern in a way that did not suggest either anger or fear.

"I guess we both made some mistakes," Donetta said. "And we both made some money. I think it's fair that you pay me more, but my lawyer says I probably can't make you. I should have paid more attention. I hope you decide to pay me something."

They sat there looking at each other, and I asked if they wanted to go back to their rooms to talk privately with their lawyers.

After several minutes, I returned to Donetta's room.

"I can't believe you told him that I said you'd probably lose," her lawyer said.

"Well, it was true," she said. "I had an excuse as a young woman for not looking at the contract, but not looking for twenty years is on me."

I left them and walked to Vern's room.

"I can't believe she admitted she'd lose and that it was partly her own fault," Vern said. "I should have contacted her sooner, but I didn't. Tell her that I'll agree to pay her for another five years."

Donetta and her lawyer accepted the offer without asking for more.

The lawyers did their jobs and privately admitted what they thought the legal outcome would be. They were confident enough to let their clients talk without them. That is not always a good idea, and I rarely suggest it. In this case it worked.

Donetta and Vern each accepted some responsibility for what happened. At their core they defined "fair" differently, but being thought of as fair was important to both of them. Donetta's disarming honesty in admitting her responsibility allowed Vern to admit he was not perfect either. Legally he did not have to pay her, according to the contract, but he also wanted what was fair.

Not all admissions of responsibility result in agreements, but it is surprising how many times people want to be thought of as reasonable and fair. It is far easier to take responsibility when it is your choice to do so than when someone tries to force you to. Donetta's admission of a weak legal argument and personal responsibility opened a door for Vern to do something he would never have otherwise considered.

My "Five Percent"... or Much, Much More

When deeply invested in righteousness with someone or some issue we care about, the idea of accepting responsibility is easy to leave on the cutting-room floor. Blame, excuses, and defensiveness are all easier to summon as we attempt to protect ourselves. There have been times when I was totally blind to my own part of a problem until someone was willing to point it out in a moment when I could hear it.

This is my last story of the chapter, and naturally it involves Patty. We have been married for more than three decades, and we have had countless opportunities to practice positively or negatively engaging in conflict. We have done both. Relationships in the home offer many opportunities to improve your conflict-engagement skills.

Patty and I were about a dozen years into our marriage, and we were struggling. Patty was home with our three daughters, who were two, four, and six years old. A sociologist friend of mine says that couples with young children often cite this as among the most difficult times in a marriage. We were right in the middle of the bell curve of frustration and discontent.

While Patty stayed home with the girls, I left early each morning to go to the office. Twelve-hour days were not uncommon for me. But I thought only of *my* twelve-hour days, not of Patty's. I was tired, Patty was tired, and our girls were tired.

I spent my days with adults. I had an office where I could shut the door, and there were people there to help me with my work. I took breaks whenever I wanted. Patty had to be on the clock from the time the girls got up until they went to bed.

When I got home, I walked into what felt like mayhem. Patty was looking for a relief pitcher, and I wanted to offer unhelpful coaching tips. I felt entitled to do what I wanted—lie on the couch and watch TV. I greatly valued my contributions to the family and wanted to be coddled. Patty had little interest in coddling her grown-up husband after corralling three young girls all day. If you had asked me what I thought, I could have given you a long and dramatic description of all I was doing, along with what more Patty could be doing.

Around this time, my friend Michael invited me out for a sandwich and a friendly chat. It was later in the evening, and the restaurant was mostly empty. We picked up our sandwiches at the counter and sat down. Before either of us had taken a bite, I began to complain.

"I come home at night to Patty and the girls," I started, oblivious to how self-centered I sounded. "She hardly notices me. She and the girls have already eaten, so I have to fend for myself for dinner. And the house is always a wreck. Everything is chaos, and she wants me to help."

I continued on, detailing the unfairness of juggling my workload and then coming home to what I felt was a disaster. I was embarrassingly unaware that this was *our* family. These were *our* daughters. This was the life *we* had chosen.

Once my monologue tapered off, Michael looked at me for a moment. "Are you done?"

I was taken aback by the fact he hadn't commiserated with what I felt was a very raw deal. I shrugged, beginning to think this wasn't going the way I'd expected.

"I think so," I said.

Michael nodded, then got right to it. "For the purposes of this conversation, Sam, I'm willing to accept that Patty is ninety-five percent of the problem; from this point forward, we're only going to talk about your five percent."

I was dumbfounded. But Michael had presented it in such a way that I couldn't argue. Patty was not to blame for a hundred percent of our problems, and saying so would be ludicrous.

We hear a lot about "aha moments," and this was mine. It was like a scene from a movie; it felt as if the sky opened up, right there in that deli, revealing that whatever conflict I find myself in, I am always part of it. No matter what fraction of "rightness" I possess, I can't say I'm blameless—ever. But more than that, Michael's statement helped me see that my part of the problem, however big or small, was the only part I could do anything about.

It has been over two decades since I had that conversation, and I can still see the restaurant and feel my face flush with embarrassment. Without my friend's willingness to be brutally honest, I would have continued to invest in my own righteous anger, with no appreciation for Patty and to the detriment (maybe even the end) of our marriage.

Takeaway

Accepting responsibility takes wisdom. Accepting responsibility requires us to face the reality of our contribution to the conflict and then make a choice about a skillful way to respond. Wanting someone else to change for us to feel better is a common feeling, but an unhelpful one when we are in a disagreement or conflict. Taking responsibility is rarely at the top of our minds. Whenever we notice ourselves getting angrier and angrier at someone's refusal to change, it is an ideal time to stop and consider how *we* can change. In the end, it is truly the only part of a conflict over which we have control.

Action

The next time you find yourself arguing with someone, try one or all of these three things:

1. Decide whether the issue is important enough to invest in the disagreement. If not, then stop arguing and move on.

2. If it is important enough to continue, try saying this: "Whatever I'm doing is not helping us be productive. I'm sorry. Is there anything I can do to make this go better?"

3. Try to concretely think about some things you like about the other person, respect about the other person, or agree with the other person about.

13

Standing Up For Yourself

When people tell me that they "avoid conflict like the plague," what I hear is that the fear of conflict itself stirs up such discomfort that they would rather either avoid it entirely or give in to what the other person wants. But even when avoiders successfully evade conflict, they sometimes flagellate themselves for not engaging. If you are an avoider and a self-flagellator (and we all are sometimes), then pain or discomfort is unavoidable, and you may be able to partially choose your pain: engagement or regret. However, choose it carefully. This is not an exact science, and what looks like self-defense to one person looks like surrendering to another.

There are three key decisions to make if you are going to give your best effort at standing up for yourself:

1. Whether the conflict is *important* enough for you to engage in it

2. Whether the circumstances are *safe* for you to engage in it

3. What the *action* is for positive engagement if you do engage in it

Jennifer Makes a Choice

Jennifer and Troy work in adjoining cubicles and do statistical analysis for their company. Jennifer is quiet and self-contained. Troy is loud and extroverted. Jennifer and Troy both do good work and receive excellent evaluations.

Jennifer goes home each night exhausted from how hard she has to work to tune out Troy's many conversations with coworkers. She feels like she has two full-time jobs—statistical analysis and tuning out Troy.

Troy gets energized by the conversations he has with friends in the office and enjoys socializing at work.

Jennifer likes her job but not her work environment. She does not dislike Troy; she just dislikes how loud he is next to her. Jennifer hates conflict, but she is considering whether to engage in conflict with Troy about her difficulties working while he carries on conversations in their workspace. She's in that classic position where, whether she engages or not, pain is unavoidable, and she longs for a fantasy option: Troy changes his behavior or leaves without Jennifer having to do anything about it. She has patiently waited for option F, but it has not materialized.

So let's look at the three questions to consider when standing up for ourselves.

#1: Is the conflict important enough for Jennifer to engage in it with Troy?

Jennifer's BATCE—best alternative to conflict engagement—so far has been to try to accept Troy's behavior and not be bothered by it. She has talked to friends, she has meditated, she has put in earplugs, she has taken antianxiety medication prescribed by a doctor. None of those have changed the level of effort it takes to do her job with Troy next to her.

Jennifer's peace of mind is at stake. The stress of trying to concentrate in a distracting environment negatively affects Jennifer's long-term ability to do her job, her relationship with her partner—whom she complains to about Troy—her status with her boss and her coworkers, her feelings about herself, and her feelings about Troy if she says something or if she doesn't. She has stopped exercising and sometimes overmedicates. The stakes are high, so the conflict is important to engage in.

#2: Are the circumstances safe for Jennifer to engage in the conflict with Troy?

To help her decide whether the circumstances are safe, Jennifer asks herself three key questions:

1. What does she want?

2. What are her fears and concerns?

3. What tradeoffs is she willing to make?

Jennifer's answers:

1. Jennifer wants to keep her job and have Troy change without her intervention. That is fantasy.

2. She fears that if she does not engage Troy, her performance and her mental health will deteriorate. Jennifer fears that if Troy does not change, she will need to find another job in a difficult economy. She fears that Troy will respond negatively if she engages with him about it, and that will make her situation worse. Jennifer also fears that she will "hate" herself if she does not stand up for herself.

3. Jennifer considers her tradeoffs. If she does nothing, then nothing will change. Yet talking to Troy scares her. It feels like a fundamental risk to her security. Alternatively, doing nothing threatens her security because she does not think she can go on like this. Not engaging also threatens her self-esteem because she does not like that she is so afraid of conflict, and she feels like she never stands up for herself.

Jennifer is in a position where she is asking herself whether she can accept Troy's behavior and get over *her* resentment or whether she needs to confront Troy and risk the possibility of him not getting over *his* resentment. She cannot control whether Troy goes to their boss to complain about Jennifer's "unreasonable" complaints.

Jennifer needs the job, and the economy is not good for finding a new job now. She decides that engaging with Troy, though unappealing, is her best option. Now she needs to create a plan to talk to Troy. The thought of having the conversation makes her sick to her stomach, but so does quitting.

There is an element of uncertainty and disappointing outcomes, but after considering all the tradeoffs and her circumstances, Jennifer decides that engaging the conflict is safe.

#3: What is the action for Jennifer to positively engage in conflict with Troy?

Jennifer faces an uncertain outcome and is about to enter a negotiation with someone who is likely to be surprised by it. She remembers hearing somewhere that if you want someone to change, then *make it as easy as possible for them to do what you want them to do.*

Jennifer also remembers hearing that when people are surprised or feel attacked or threatened, they often respond defensively and don't do their best listening or thinking. Further, people like to help solve other people's problems. Is there some way she can make this not about Troy personally and also not selfishly about her?

It is a tall order. So she turns to Robert Cialdini's work on influence.[1] Cialdini and his colleagues identify six principles of influence—likability, reciprocity, scarcity, commitment, social proof, and authority. How many of these might she be able to hit in her conversation with Troy?

---

1 Roselle Wissler, Robert B. Cialdini, and N. J. Schweitzer, "The Science of Influence: Using Six Principles of Persuasion to Negotiate and Mediate More Effectively," *Dispute Resolution Magazine* 9, no. 2 (Fall 2002): 14–22.

She and Troy have worked next to each other for two years and have never had a harsh word. They are about the same age, they're divorced, and they've talked some about the struggles of shared custody of children. They are both avid fans of musical theater and occasionally talk about new shows. Jennifer thinks that while they are not close, they have some similarities. She is OK as far as *likability* goes.

Because they have shown mutual respect, she thinks there is *reciprocity*. Troy is louder and more of an extrovert, but they have always shared things well and cooperated in meetings. Even when they have disagreed about how something might be done, there has not seemed to be any resentment. Troy has shown a willingness to listen, and Jennifer thinks she has done the same.

Scarcity is in the job and the relationship itself. Troy wants to be liked, and seems generally to be a people pleaser. That is a double-edged sword because Troy might be a little embarrassed about having been unaware that his loud personal conversations are so difficult for Jennifer. She needs to approach this carefully, but she can point out that this is an issue that only she and Troy can solve, so there is scarcity and reason for both of them to be influenced.

Commitment is something that Jennifer appreciates about Troy. He comes to work on time and gets his work done. When they are on teams and split tasks, they are both good about completing the jobs and sharing responsibilities. She has kept commitments to Troy, and his word has always been good to her. There is some trust.

Social proof is a bit difficult because everybody likes Troy, but she is the only one who works in such close proximity with him. Others might hear his conversations, but not with the same frequency or at the same decibel level. Jennifer is also concerned about bringing in any issues that suggest that she has been complaining to coworkers (she has not). That might make Troy defensive. She thinks on this issue she might have to own that she has more difficulty than some in concentrating when the environment is loud. She might compare it to why some people with offices close their doors—not to keep others out, but because they are unable to avoid being distracted by people walking by in the hallway. The people walking by aren't doing anything wrong; the person in the office is just unusually prone to distraction. Social proof goes to what others similarly situated are doing. The social proof might be embedded in the rest of the principles because they are in an environment where people seem to care about each other.

Authority is the final principle of influence, and Jennifer's only authority is in her job performance, her pleasant demeanor, and her own support for others. Everyone, including Troy, knows that she is good at what she does and is willing to share what she knows without arrogance or complaint.

This may seem to be a long analysis, but this is a potentially life-changing conversation for Jennifer. Can she keep her job, income, and health, or does she need to find another place to work, which isn't a promising option right now?

Jennifer runs her plan by a friend and decides to have a conversation with Troy. When no one else is around, she goes to Troy's cubicle and says, "Troy, I've been struggling with something and wondered if you'd be willing to let me treat you to lunch to pick your brain?"

We all like to be asked for our wisdom, and Troy quickly says yes. Jennifer is grateful when Troy does not ask for details.

Jennifer knows that Troy likes Italian food, so she picks an Italian restaurant close by, and they sit across from each other in a booth with a red-checked tablecloth.

Jennifer begins, "Troy, you are probably the best-liked person in our office, and I'm lucky to be working on the same team as you. Sometimes I wish I was as easy a conversationalist as you are."

She pauses for Troy to hear the compliment.

"For the last several months, I've had more and more trouble concentrating. When people come by your desk to talk, I just can't block it out and do my work. I'm leaving work more exhausted and coming into work anxious." She gathered her breath and went on.

"I've been afraid to have this conversation because I don't think you're doing anything wrong, and I'm a little embarrassed that I haven't been able to just do my job and ignore what's going on next to me."

She made it a point to look at Troy and did her best not to complain about him.

"Do you mind if I share with you what I've done to try to adjust to it and then hear any thoughts that you have?"

Troy looked surprised but not particularly defensive.

"It's gotten so difficult that I've seen a therapist, begun meditating, changed my diet, and even tried medication. None of it has worked. The last thing I wanted to do was talk to you about changing anything *you're* doing just to help me, but I've run out of ideas. I've been nervous even to have this conversation. Do you have any thoughts?"

Their food came, and Troy pushed his to the side and leaned in to talk to Jennifer.

"First, let me say that I'm sorry work has become so difficult for you," Troy began. "You've hidden it well because your work continues to be great. You're not the first person in my life to tell me that I talk too much and too loud." Troy laughed. "I'm embarrassed that what I saw as good-natured office banter made your job more difficult. I truly had no idea. I appreciate your honesty. This must have been really hard for you. You must have been thinking about this for a long time. Before I start spouting off my solutions, I'd like to hear yours."

Jennifer and Troy regained their appetites and spent the rest of the lunch talking about some ways for Troy to enjoy his extroverted ways that were not so disruptive to Jennifer doing her job in a more introverted way.

They discussed taking lunch at different times, offsetting their lunch breaks, and starting the workday at different times. They decided that lengthy conversations would move to the breakroom. Tom even suggested a code word Jennifer could use when she was really struggling. Jennifer laughed, but appreciated such a practical suggestion. Jennifer offered to make a better effort to enjoy the fact that one of the reasons Troy and others had these "distracting" conversations was because their work environment was so good, and people genuinely liked one another.

Not everyone is as careful as Jennifer or as hesitant to speak up. Not everyone is as perceptive as Troy about how some of their strengths can also be weaknesses.

Had Troy responded defensively and been unwilling to discuss solutions, Jennifer would have made her best effort to step into a scary situation without the bonus outcome. It happens. She would have gained the clarity that Troy was not going to be part of the solution, and she'd need to find a way to accept her work environment exactly as it existed or find another job.

Jennifer felt good about not running from the conflict, and she got the bonus outcome with a collaborative partner. Had Troy been a loud, angry person, she might have made a different decision about what it looked like to stand up for herself. But she would have stepped into the discomfort to find out—not an easy choice. She accepted that a pain-free option was unavailable.

A Good "No" Has Great Value

Here is one simple way to stand up for yourself. If you have considered the alternative to what the other person is asking of you, and you decide that the alternative is better than saying yes to the request, then just say no. Nothing more and no explanation. Put the responsibility on them to tell you why you should do what they want.

If the other person refuses to accept "no," then you can sit there and do nothing. Their discomfort does not have to be yours to solve. You can leave the room. You can end the Zoom meeting or hang up the phone. "No" is an incredibly powerful tool that shifts the anxiety to someone else to either accept your "no" or offer something that you might be open to hear.

If you are a people pleaser, it will be uncomfortable for you to say no and even more uncomfortable not to explain it. If nothing else, it will be an experiment to learn that you can be OK behaving in a different yet principled way. You may also find that your refusing to do what someone else wants is not as big a deal as you think it is. Sometimes we give ourselves too much credit for the impact we have on a situation. It is a valuable tool to add to your kit of conflict engagement.

If you choose to take this path, it is still important to do the work in the previous section. You will want to consider whether the issue is important enough to say yes *or* no, and you will want to consider whether each answer is safe. If it is important *and* safe, then you can consider what action to take. The action may be to do nothing and say no with your behavior. Another action is to look someone in the eye and say no.

Had Troy said no to Jennifer in our previous story, the outcome would have been different. Had Carlos said no to his racist supervisor in chapter 9, the outcome would have been different. The circumstances were very different for Troy and Carlos in that Troy was invited to be part of a solution in a skilled way. Carlos was experiencing abusive and possibly illegal behavior.

The consequences were important to Carlos, but he decided that saying no and calling out his supervisor was not safe, based on his and his wife's evaluation of their circumstances, even though his boss's behavior was indefensible. In its own way, Carlos's choice was also a courageous one because it was a conscious decision to face his reality and create a plan where he might say no to the whole job once his wife was back at work. How we respond is profoundly personal.

There are times, however, when just saying no changes the entire dynamic, but we don't always know how. Eunice was the chief probation officer of a staff of fifty other officers. The officers had three levels of titles—officer, senior officer, and supervising officer. The titles were largely allocated based on years of service. The culture of the office was to arrive at least a half hour before the eight o'clock opening bell and to stay after the five o'clock designated end of the workday. Arriving early and staying late was an indication of being a "hard worker."

Everyone got lockstep raises based on their starting pay when they began and any governmental edicts for raises. There was no extra pay for arriving early and staying late.

Skip was finishing his sixth year on the staff and going in for his annual evaluation. He arrived on time and left on time, but he did not come early or stay late. His tenure qualified him to be a senior officer, but the title was irrelevant to him.

"How do you think you're doing?" Eunice began as she looked at the standard questionnaire all employees completed before their review.

"It's all there," Skip said pleasantly. "I think I do my job well, but I'm not auditioning to run the department."

"That's part of what I wanted to talk to you about," Eunice said. "I'm not going to be here forever, and you have some of the skills that might make you a good leader."

"Thank you, Eunice," Skip said. "But I'm serious, I don't want to lead the office."

"Some things you need to consider," Eunice continued, ignoring what Skip had just said, "are getting here earlier and staying later. Sometimes your desk is pretty messy, too."

"I get it, but I'm not bucking for the job," Skip repeated, getting a little irritated. "Am I not getting my caseload finished?"

"You're handling more cases than most, and your files are impeccable."

"Will I be paid more for coming in early and staying late?" Skip asked.

"No, you get the same government rate based on time and grade."

"Then I'm confused," Skip said. "I don't want to be the leader, my work is good, I won't get paid more, and yet you want me to come in early and stay late for a promotion that I don't want, right?"

"Exactly," Eunice said, as if she were having a conversation with someone who was not in the room.

"No," Skip said, "but thank you. Anything else?"

"I guess not," Eunice said, dumbfounded that Skip wanted something different from what she wanted.

Not everyone would have felt as comfortable as Skip. He cared about doing his job well and treating his clients on probation with respect. Skip's real passion, however, was hiking with his husband, Robert, and their dog, Rocky. Being a probation officer paid well enough, and it offered Skip the regular hours he wanted. Whatever benefit he might have gotten from longer hours and less hiking was not worth it. He had no passion for or curiosity about running a probation office.

Skip informally considered the questions about importance, safety, and action regarding engaging in this conflict, without writing them out on a piece of paper. The job was not important enough to work harder at it, and saying no to Eunice was worth the conflict with her expectations. It was safe because he was doing good work and did not fear repercussions. The engagement was a short and sweet "no." He did not explain his reasons to Eunice, but he did ask her questions that might have led her to see that whatever she had to offer did not interest him. The anxiety of finding a new chief officer was shifted completely to Eunice. It was her job, and Skip had no interest in doing it.

Saying no to a boss can be hard, even if your position is secure, and there are those of us for whom such a simple "no" might have been difficult. Many of us would want to explain exactly why we did not want the job so that we would be liked. We might give excuses for why saying no did not make us failed human beings.

Some of us might even want to take on helping Eunice find a replacement. There is nothing wrong with doing those things, but only if you want to, and if by saying yes to those activities you are not saying no to more important ones, whether they involve birdwatching with your partner or getting home to unwind with a ginger ale while you watch TV with your cat.

It can be intimidating to say no to someone else's expectations, and if there's a conflict, someone has an expectation.

A Nurse Stands Up

Standing up for yourself can involve doing something to stand up for others. This final perspective on standing up for yourself involves my mother and a controversial issue. My mom was in her forties when she had an opportunity to work with Planned Parenthood. She was trained as a nurse and had worked for the visiting nurses' association in poor parts of Indianapolis in the 1950s to help people who did not have the mobility or means to get the medical care they needed. She later married my dad, and they had two children—my brother and me. When my brother and I were teenagers, we moved to a small farming community.

Mom is deeply committed to the Christian faith she learned as a child growing up in the Midwest. Her commitment, however, is personal and not something she requires anyone else to believe. Nor does she believe it is her right or her job to judge people who believe differently from her. She would not qualify for any popular definition of "evangelical" that shows up in polls or cable news channels. That is not her way of standing up, though it may be for others.

Mom was influenced by her own circumstances growing up. She was born near the end of the Great Depression and lost her only sister and her father by the time she was eighteen years old. Her mother, my grandmother, worked to run a coal yard by herself in the late 1940s and early 1950s, when women often could not get bank loans. My grandmother also ran a boarding house, where one of their boarders committed suicide in his room.

Mom was not a stranger to sadness, financial hardship, or deep commitment to principles. She was also not a stranger to difficult life circumstances and nuanced problems that were not easily solved. She believed that the most difficult problems require that people who disagree engage, listen, and compromise, even about very important and principled differences.

In the late 1970s, Mom was asked to work part-time for Planned Parenthood, in a space donated by a local church. Mom was strongly opposed to abortion, but she also remembered her nurse's training when women, attempting do-it-yourself abortions, died as a result of their desperation. Sometimes the child and mother were both lost in those circumstances. Her views about sex and marriage were not more important than the people she thought she could help.

She did not want any woman to be pregnant who did not want to be. She thought that the most effective thing she could do was to provide sex education and contraception to young women and men so that women, and even girls, could avoid unwanted pregnancies. She could find no better place than Planned Parenthood to help women take care of themselves.

I would not ask that you agree with my mother on issues of faith, family planning, or abortion. She still opposes abortion and wants women not to choose it, but she believes in their right to choose it. She felt that standing up for women who were vulnerable was also standing up for herself. She said no to some in her faith community and others in her social circles. She said no to a simplified view of the issue that offered only binary, closed-minded thinking. She was willing to be criticized and even ostracized for her commitment. For her, engaging in this conflict was important, and not always safe, but safe enough to take her stand. The action she took was to work in an organization that helped people in need, even if she did not agree with the organization about everything it did.

There are many things about which my mom and I have disagreed over the years, but I have never doubted her compassionate commitment to be kind, thoughtful, and respectful to people who look different from how she looks, believe differently than she does, and live their lives differently than she does.

Takeaway

Standing up for yourself does not look the same for everyone. Sometimes standing up for yourself is a dramatic and risky action. At other times, standing up for yourself is recognizing your circumstances and thoughtfully creating a plan. Yet another way to stand up for yourself is to stand up for others, even as you pay a price for doing it.

Action

When you feel the unpleasant tug of someone else's conflict, even if it is someone arguing in the hallway, resist your urge to turn around and avoid it. Walk down the hall past the conflict and pay attention to it, not as a gawker at a roadside accident but with purpose. After you walk by, consider how it made you feel, how long the feeling lasted, and whether you learned anything from it. Was your response proportional to what was happening? Then see whether you think your own discomfort might have been greater than the discomfort felt by the people who were arguing. Was one of them standing up for themselves in a way that you wish you would sometimes do?

Conclusion

In writing this book, I wanted to point out that conflict is not just about wars, elections, and divorces. Rather, it is a normal part of everyday life. As such, it behooves us to do conflict better.

We cannot always choose when or how conflict will appear, but we can be sure it will. By practicing positive conflict engagement rather than thoughtless conflict reaction, we have some choice in how we respond to conflict. When conflict comes knocking, we can choose to answer the door or not. If we decide to answer, we can choose whether to invite the conflict in. If we invite it in, we can consider whether we want to offer it a seat at our table. Dinner can be a cold snack or a full-course meal. We can see what dish conflict has brought to the potluck and whether we want to sample the offering. There are foods we reject, are allergic to, or have never tried, and we can decide what positive engagement looks like.

The stories in this book offer a peek into our constant relationship with conflict. Having someone intervene in my own relationship with conflict literally saved my life. I stopped drinking, but that was only the appetizer. Conflict informs all our relationships, and in my case, a relationship with alcohol was just one of them. Although I refer to conflict as a thing, it is always a relationship, a synergistic experience that is affected by how you think about your circumstances. And how others think about theirs.

Your relationship with conflict is not a reason for blame, shame, embarrassment, or regret. We are human beings facing our reality. Sometimes your best effort or the effort of another person is insufficient for a positive interaction. Other times you may be astounded by how graciously you chose to respond to someone who acted poorly. If you pay attention, you will experience moments when someone treats you with kindness and generosity in spite of your own imperfect behavior. Those unexpected flashes of connection can be remarkable.

But no matter how accepting we are of conflict as a fact of life, it still causes discomfort, so we do not prefer it. Option F is the alluring fantasy in our heads that leads us to believe that by avoiding it, we'll dispense with it. My invitation is to engage with conflict. This means learning to recognize it, thoughtfully considering your options for whether and how to engage with it, and, as much as possible, treating ourselves and others with generosity and compassion. Sometimes your generosity and compassion will be met with anger and unkindness. You can adjust and take care of yourself. You will not always get the results you wish for when you choose to engage. And you will sometimes fall short in your expectations of how you want to respond. However, until you reach the end of your days, you will always have more chances to practice, and some resolutions will feel good.

You may not agree with what it means to resolve conflict, and you may not agree that some conflicts aren't resolvable in the moment. Then again, all conflicts will ultimately resolve because we all will die. As fatalistic as that sounds, it is not something to forget. As we suffer through righteous anger, resentment, entitlement, and unmet expectations, we can choose how long we want to keep our focus there. With practice, we can turn our gaze to other vistas and open ourselves to outcomes that aren't always clean and tidy but sometimes opaque and messy. Messy can be beautiful, despite or even because of the different lenses we have chosen to try on.

Conflict does not require us to keep score, though it is enticing to do so. Conflict does not require us to judge other people, but it is tempting to form opinions. Scorekeeping and judging prolong conflict. If we are going to keep score and pass judgment, that is our right, but we need to own the consequences to ourselves and others.

Alternatively, we can choose to change our perception about and improve our relationship with conflict. When we are conflicted within ourselves, we can learn to live with our imperfections and accept that they are part of us, not all of us. When we are in conflict with someone else, we can do the hard work of listening. We won't always get what we want, but that is not necessarily a loss. Change is inevitable and growth is possible. And the byproduct of engaging conflict is not always immediately apparent, but it is full of hopeful prospects.

You now know more about my personal life than you ever wanted to. I've made many mistakes. But I hope you've gained some insight into what it takes to engage with conflict in a positive and productive way. I am thrilled to have had you along for the journey. Whether you've been reading this book to help you deal with tensions in a work setting or to work through issues in your personal relationships, it is my sincere wish that you have found at least one way to think or respond differently to conflict.

When you take the plunge into engaging in conflict with courage, compassion, and wisdom, remarkable things can happen. The next time you find yourself in the midst of conflict, I hope you'll pause, experience the discomfort, listen, accept responsibility for your part in it, and respond thoughtfully rather than react reflexively. Again, you may not always get the outcome you want, but you will learn that you can be OK, and perhaps even thrive, in spite of a disappointing result.

Listen to your justice gene, but don't surrender to it. Hold on to your principles, but don't claim that people who believe differently are necessarily evil. Be prudent and safe, but don't give in to your instinct to default to comfort when discomfort can teach you so much.

Ask yourself hard questions about why you feel the need to be "right," and what's the worst that could happen if you're wrong. Work on identifying the drivers of your own conflicts, and develop your skills for recognizing, pausing, and choosing before reacting. Practice confidence and humility, and never stop trying to act wisely.

So many stories in this book involve my wife, Patty. It seems only natural to end with one. Our daughter, Rachel, and our son-in-law, Ben, have two young sons who are one and three years old. Rachel taught school for years but now stays home with the boys. Ben leaves home each morning for his job. When Ben returns at five or six in the evening, he and Rachel are both exhausted and want support and a break. It is often not available, and their resilience tanks are frequently empty. Conflict sits waiting on both their shoulders.

Patty and I have a policy passed down from our own parents not to offer unsolicited advice. Sometimes we hold to that policy better than other times. And occasionally a question is put to us. As we were leaving after a visit, Ben and Rachel asked if we had any suggestions for how to manage their end-of-day struggles.

Patty said, "If you end the day each assuming that the other person had a harder day than you did, you'll find a way to work it out."

Then we left. Patty did not explain how to carry out her advice or what exactly she meant.

Perhaps that is the best advice I can give you when you step into conflict. Rather than focusing on how hard it is for you, consider how hard it is for the other person. And offer yourself the same kindness by acknowledging the frustration of your own internal conflicts without beating yourself up. Those two things by themselves are revolutionary approaches.

Good luck and best wishes.